Welcome to Your Journey Home to Yourself

This journal is more than pages —
it's a sacred space to meet yourself again and again.
Each day is an invitation to pause, breathe, and reconnect.

Through daily rituals, mindful meals,
journaling, and gratitude,
you'll create harmony between doing and being,
and learn to live with greater awareness, ease,
and flow.
There is no rush.
Transformation is not linear — it spirals and
expands,
bringing you back to yourself with deeper grace
each time.

.

How to Use This Journal

Begin wherever you are—this journey unfolds in
divine timing.
Each day includes five simple anchors:

- Affirmation—a phrase to set your energy.
- Morning Ritual—a grounding or awakening
  practice.
- Meal & Movement—a cue to honor your body's
  rhythm.
- Journal Reflection—questions to deepen
  awareness.
- Evening Gratitude—a gentle close to your day.

💛 Remember

This journey isn't about perfection
—
it's about presence.
It's about grace, self-love,
and creating space for joy every day.

May this year bring you peace,
clarity, and radiant transformation.

My Intention for This
Year of Transformation:

_____

_____

_____

DAY 1—GROUND & PRESENCE
"I am rooted and calm".

MORNING RITUAL

Sit comfortably with both feet flat on the floor.

Take three slow, deep breaths,

Feel your connection to the earth beneath you.

Let each exhale soften your shoulders and your mind.

MEAL & MOVEMENT

Begin your journey with grounding comfort — nourish with root-based, earthy meals like roasted sweet potatoes or warm quinoa bowls. Move with presence — flow through gentle yoga or take a barefoot walk to feel supported by the earth beneath you.

Today I nourish my body with:

_____

Today I move with intention through:

_____

"I am safe. I am steady. I am supported."

JOURNAL REFLECTION

What does stability feel like in my body today?

Where in my life am I craving more grounding?

EVENING GRATITUDE

One moment that made me feel peaceful today:

_____

_____

DAY 2 – GROUND & PRESENCE

"I am rooted in peace."

MORNING RITUAL

Before reaching for your phone, take three mindful breaths. Sit quietly with your hands over your heart and repeat: "I am where I am meant to be."
As you breathe, feel the rise and fall of your chest —

a reminder that you are supported by every breath, every beat, every moment.
(Use this ritual to start your day with trust and grounded intention.)
.

MEAL & MOVEMENT

Tip: Choose foods that grow from the earth and movements that connect you to your body — walking, stretching, or dancing barefoot.

Today I nourish my body with:

_____

Today I move with intention through:

_____

JOURNAL REFLECTION

Where in my life am I trying to rush the process?
What would it feel like to trust the timing of my growth?
(Allow yourself to notice if impatience or control are showing up — and gently breathe through them.)

_____

*"Stillness is strength.
I trust life's timing."*

EVENING GRATITUDE

One moment that reminded me to trust was

_____

DAY 3-GROUND & PRESENCE
"I am supported in all I do."

MORNING RITUAL
Take a few moments to stand tall with your feet firmly planted on the floor. Close your eyes and visualize gentle roots extending from your feet into the earth. With every inhale, imagine drawing up strength and stability. With every exhale, release tension and doubt into the ground. Whisper softly:
"I am supported. I am steady. I am safe."
(This short grounding practice is a reminder that your stability comes from within.)

_____

_____

JOURNAL REFLECTION
Where do I resist receiving support — and why?
What would it feel like to trust that I don't have to carry everything alone?
(Let this reflection open your awareness to the invisible networks — people, energy, and divine timing — that hold you daily.)

_____

_____

MEAL & MOVEMENT
Choose grounding foods — root vegetables, whole grains, warm teas. Move in ways that remind you of strength — yoga poses like Mountain, Warrior, or Tree.

Today I nourish my body with:

_____

Today I move with intention through:

_____

*"I am held.
I am supported. I am safe."*

EVENING GRATITUDE
One person or experience that supported me today was:

_____

_____

DAY 4-GROUND & PRESENCE
"Simplicity brings peace."

MORNING RITUAL

Before you begin your day, take a look around your space.

Choose one small area — your desk, nightstand, or kitchen counter.

Take five mindful minutes to clear it. As you do, breathe deeply and silently repeat: "As I create space around me, I create peace within me."

When you're done, pause for a moment and simply feel the stillness you've created.

(This practice teaches that small, intentional actions anchor calm and order within.)

_____

_____

JOURNAL REFLECTION

Where in my life am I holding on to more than I need? What one small thing can I release today to make room for peace?

(This reflection helps you connect minimalism with inner stability — releasing clutter to make space for calm.)

_____

_____

MEAL & MOVEMENT

Opt for simple, wholesome meals — one-bowl nourishment, warm soups, or herbal teas. Move slowly — a mindful stretch, short walk, or gentle yoga flow — noticing each movement with presence.

Today I nourish my body with:

_____

Today I move with intention through:

_____

"I honor small beginnings. Peace fills the space I create."

EVENING GRATITUDE
Today I created peace by letting go of:

_____

_____

DAY 5-GROUND & PRESENCE
"Presence is my power."

MORNING RITUAL
Before beginning your tasks today, take five mindful breaths.

With each inhale, say silently: "I am here."

With each exhale, say: "Now."

Repeat this cycle until you feel your body settle into calm awareness.

When your mind wanders, gently return to the rhythm of your breath.

Allow the simplicity of this moment to be enough.

(This short ritual awakens your inner presence — where peace naturally lives.)

JOURNAL REFLECTION
How often do I move through the day on autopilot?

How can I bring more awareness to simple daily actions like breathing, walking, or eating?

(Presence doesn't require more time — only more awareness. Today's journaling brings mindfulness into ordinary moments.)

MEAL & MOVEMENT
Try a mindful meal — no screens, no distractions, just presence with each bite. For movement, practice "walking in awareness" — noticing your steps, breath, and surroundings with full attention.

Today I nourish my body with:

Today I move with intention through:

"Presence is my power."

EVENING GRATITUDE
A moment I felt truly present today was:

TRUEJOY-LIVING
A YEAR OF TRANSFORMATION

DAY 6-GROUND & PRESENCE
"I find peace in stillness."

MORNING RITUAL

Begin your day in silence — no phone, no noise, no rush.
Sit or stand near a window and gaze softly outside.
Notice the stillness between sounds, the pause between breaths.
For three minutes, let yourself simply be.
When your mind drifts, gently return to that space of quiet within you.
Whisper: "In stillness, I meet myself."
(This practice helps you reconnect to your inner calm — the place that's always there beneath movement and thought.)

JOURNAL REFLECTION

When was the last time I allowed myself to rest without guilt?
What happens inside me when I stop doing and start being?
(Stillness is where alignment happens — today's journaling brings awareness to the peace that already lives within you.)

MEAL & MOVEMENT

Choose warm, grounding meals that invite comfort — like oatmeal, soups, or roasted vegetables. Move slowly and intentionally — gentle yoga, deep stretching, or slow walking — savoring every movement.

Today I nourish my body with:

_____

Today I move with intention through:

_____

"Peace is always within reach."

EVENING GRATITUDE
A quiet moment I appreciated today:

_____

_____

DAY 7-GROUND & PRESENCE
"I honor my natural rhythm."

MORNING RITUAL

Begin your day by tuning in to your body before tuning in to the world.
Sit quietly and place one hand on your heart, the other on your belly.
Take three deep breaths and ask yourself:
"What do I need most today — movement, stillness, nourishment, or rest?"
Let your breath answer before your mind does.
Once you feel your inner guidance, set one gentle intention to honor it.
(This ritual reconnects you to your body's wisdom — your truest compass.)

JOURNAL REFLECTION

How does my body communicate its needs to me?
Where in my life am I being called to slow down — or speed up — in alignment with my natural rhythm?
(Let your journaling be gentle and curious. Awareness begins with listening.)

MEAL & MOVEMENT

Honor your body's rhythm — choose meals that match your energy today, light and fresh if you feel open, warm and hearty if you need grounding. Move intuitively — stretch, sway, or rest as your body guides you, trusting its natural flow.

Today I nourish my body with:

_____

Today I move with intention through:

_____

"When I flow with life, peace flows through me."

EVENING GRATITUDE

One way I honored my rhythm today was:

_____

_____

DAY 8–GROUND & PRESENCE

"I am grounded in gratitude."

MORNING RITUAL

Begin your day by naming three things you're grateful
for before you get out of bed. They can be simple — your
breath, your warm blanket, the sunrise. As you name
each one, breathe deeply and feel the warmth of
appreciation in your heart.
 Let that energy expand through your body like sunlight
spreading across the earth.
Whisper: "Thank you, life, for supporting me in all ways."
(This practice reprograms your nervous system for calm
and opens the heart to abundance.)

_____

_____

JOURNAL REFLECTION

What am I most grateful for in this season of my life?
How does gratitude shift my energy and perspective?
(Journaling through gratitude transforms awareness —
every moment becomes a teacher and a gift.)

_____

_____

MEAL & MOVEMENT

Savor each bite as an act of thanks — choose colorful,
nourishing foods and eat slowly, noticing flavor and texture.
Move in appreciation — stretch your arms wide, take a walk
outdoors, or dance to a song that makes you smile.

Today I nourish my body with:

_____

Today I move with intention through:

_____

"Gratitude roots me in joy."

EVENING GRATITUDE

One small joy I appreciated today was:

_____

_____

DAY 9-GROUND & PRESENCE
"My body is my home."

MORNING RITUAL

Upon waking, take a deep, conscious breath and thank your body for carrying you through another day of life. Stand before a mirror or close your eyes, and softly place your hands on your heart or over an area that needs love. Whisper:

"Thank you, body, for supporting me, protecting me, and grounding me in this life."

Take a moment to notice how your body feels — not to judge, but to listen. Allow gratitude to wash through you, grounding your awareness in presence and self-acceptance.

(This ritual reconnects you to your most sacred home — the body that holds your soul.)

JOURNAL REFLECTION

How have I treated my body this week — with love, or with pressure?

How can I honor my body more deeply — through rest, nourishment, or compassion?

(This reflection encourages reconnection — remembering that your body is not separate from your spirit, but its sacred vessel.)

MEAL & MOVEMENT

Choose foods that feel nurturing, not restrictive — warm, wholesome meals that remind you of comfort and safety. Move with tenderness — stretch slowly, rest intentionally, or take a gentle walk while appreciating every breath your body gives you.

Today I nourish my body with:

Today I move with intention through:

"I am safe within my body. My body is home."

EVENING GRATITUDE

One way my body supported me today was:

TRUEJOY-LIVING
A YEAR OF TRANSFORMATION

DAY 10-GROUND & PRESENCE
"I create calm within."

MORNING RITUAL

Find a quiet place to sit, close your eyes, and bring your awareness to your breath. Place one hand over your heart and the other on your abdomen. Inhale deeply through your nose for a count of 4, hold for 2, and exhale slowly for 6. Repeat this for three cycles, allowing your body to soften and your mind to settle.

With each exhale, silently repeat:

"Calm begins with me."

(This ritual centers your energy and teaches your nervous system that safety starts from within.)

JOURNAL REFLECTION

When I feel anxious or overwhelmed, what helps me return to calm?

How can I create more inner calm through small, daily choices?

(Your journal becomes a mirror for peace — each word a step closer to stillness.)

MEAL & MOVEMENT

Choose foods that soothe — herbal teas, nourishing soups, or meals rich in greens. Move gently — try a mindful stretch or slow flow yoga, focusing on each breath as a wave of calm flowing through your body.

Today I nourish my body with:

Today I move with intention through:

"I carry calm wherever I go."

EVENING GRATITUDE

A moment I felt calm today was:

DAY 11—GROUND & PRESENCE

"Consistency roots my peace."

MORNING RITUAL

Begin your day in stillness. Sit comfortably, close your eyes, and gently place one hand on your heart and one on your belly.
Breathe in through your nose for a slow count of four, hold for two, and exhale through your mouth for six.
Repeat this pattern for at least five rounds.
With every inhale, think "I receive peace."
With every exhale, think "I release tension."
Afterward, take a moment to notice how calm feels in your body.
Whisper: "With each breath, I return home to myself."
(This ritual strengthens your mind–body connection and rewires your system toward peace.)

_____

_____

JOURNAL REFLECTION

How does my breath feel when I am calm versus when I am stressed?
Where in my day can I pause to breathe with awareness?
What emotions soften when I focus on my breathing?
(Breath is the bridge between body and spirit — your journal helps you listen to what it's telling you.)

_____

_____

MEAL & MOVEMENT

Start your morning with hydration — lemon water or herbal tea. Choose light, easy-to-digest meals that allow your body to breathe freely. For movement, practice breath-led yoga or take a slow walk, matching each step to your inhale and exhale.

Today I nourish my body with:

_____

Today I move with intention through:

_____

"Peace begins with my breath."

EVENING GRATITUDE

A moment today when I remembered to breathe:

_____

_____

DAY 12—GROUND & PRESENCE
"I release what's heavy."

MORNING RITUAL

Find a quiet space where you won't be disturbed. Close your eyes, inhale deeply, and as you exhale, imagine releasing anything that feels heavy — thoughts, expectations, old stories. Visualize them leaving your body as wisps of gray mist, dissolving into the earth.

Place your hand on your heart and whisper: "I choose to release what no longer serves my peace."

Take one more slow, grounding breath and feel your body lighten with every exhale.

(This ritual clears energetic space for renewal and reconnects you to your inner calm.)

_____

_____

JOURNAL REFLECTION

What am I carrying emotionally that feels heavy or outdated?

How would I feel — physically and emotionally — if I truly let it go?

(Writing is an act of release — each word helps you empty what weighs you down and make room for light.)

_____

_____

MEAL & MOVEMENT

Support release through cleansing foods — greens, citrus, herbal teas, and water. Move gently but purposefully — try a twisting yoga flow or a long walk outdoors to encourage energetic and physical release.

Today I nourish my body with:

_____

Today I move with intention through:

_____

"As I release, I rise."

EVENING GRATITUDE

Something I released today

_____

_____

DAY 13-GROUND & PRESENCE
"I feel safe being myself.

MORNING RITUAL

Begin the morning by standing tall, feet firmly grounded on the floor.
Take three deep breaths, inhaling through your nose and exhaling slowly through your mouth. Place your hands over your heart and say aloud:
"It's safe for me to be who I am."
As you breathe, feel your heart expand with each inhale and soften with each exhale.
Visualize yourself surrounded by a gentle golden light — a shield of safety and self-acceptance.
(This ritual reminds you that you are your own safe space — acceptance begins within.)

JOURNAL REFLECTION

What parts of myself do I hide or quiet around others?
How can I create a space — inner or outer — where my true self feels welcomed?
(Journaling today allows the real you to take up space — gently, lovingly, without apology.)

MEAL & MOVEMENT

Eat meals that bring comfort and familiarity — foods that feel like home. Move in a way that expresses freedom: dance in your living room, stretch intuitively, or take a walk while breathing into your heart space.

Today I nourish my body with:

Today I move with intention through:

"I am safe. I am seen. I am enough."

EVENING GRATITUDE

One moment I showed up authentically today was:

DAY 14-GROUND & PRESENCE

"My energy is grounded and strong."

MORNING RITUAL

Find your strength in stillness. Sit or stand tall, close your eyes, and take a deep breath into your belly.

As you exhale, imagine a wave of calm moving down through your legs and feet, connecting you to the earth.

Visualize golden roots spreading from the soles of your feet deep into the ground, anchoring you firmly yet flexibly.

Repeat slowly:

"My energy is steady. My roots run deep. My presence is power."

(This ritual stabilizes your inner energy and teaches your body that true strength is calm, not forceful.)

JOURNAL REFLECTION

How does it feel in my body when my energy is grounded?

How can I protect and maintain my energy through boundaries and mindfulness?

(Your journal becomes a map for your energy — showing you where you stand tall and where you can root deeper.)

MEAL & MOVEMENT

Fuel your body with balanced, grounding meals — whole grains, lean proteins, and roasted vegetables. Move with strength and flow — yoga, Pilates, or strength-based movement that connects breath with power.

Today I nourish my body with:

_____

Today I move with intention through:

_____

"I am anchored in strength. I am steady in spirit.

EVENING GRATITUDE

A moment I felt strong and centered today:

_____

_____

DAY 15-GROUND & PRESENCE
"Stillness reconnects me to myself."

MORNING RITUAL

Begin your day in silence — before checking your phone or speaking to anyone, take five minutes to simply be.
Find a comfortable seat, close your eyes, and place your hands in your lap, palms facing upward. Notice your breath without trying to change it.
As thoughts arise, let them drift by like clouds in a calm sky. After a few moments, whisper:
"In stillness, I find myself again."
(This ritual allows the mind to quiet and the heart to speak — guiding you back to your natural rhythm.)

JOURNAL REFLECTION

What distractions or habits keep me from connecting inward?
Who am I when I let everything else fall away?
(Stillness is not emptiness — it's full of truth. Use today's reflection to rediscover what's waiting in your quiet spaces.)

MEAL & MOVEMENT

Choose peaceful nourishment — simple, light foods that don't overstimulate. Eat in silence, noticing flavor and texture. Move with intention and ease — gentle stretching or yin yoga to quiet the body and settle the mind.

Today I nourish my body with:

Today I move with intention through:

"I am whole when I am still."

EVENING GRATITUDE

A peaceful moment I created for myself today:

DAY 16-GROUND & PRESENCE
"I am connected to the Earth."

MORNING RITUAL

Step outside, even if just for a moment. Feel the air on your skin, the temperature, the sounds of life awakening around you. Stand tall, feet firmly planted on the ground, and take three slow, steady breaths. With each inhale, imagine drawing strength and nourishment up from the Earth. With each exhale, send gratitude back down through your feet.

Say quietly: "The Earth supports me, nourishes me, and grounds me in peace."

(This ritual restores your natural harmony with the world around you — grounding you in unity and calm.)

JOURNAL REFLECTION

Where do I feel most connected to the Earth — what environments bring me peace?

How can I honor the Earth more through my daily actions or mindset?

(Journaling today brings awareness to your interconnection — the Earth isn't separate from you; it's part of your being.)

MEAL & MOVEMENT

Eat close to nature — fresh fruits, leafy greens, whole grains, and clean water. Choose one meal today to enjoy outdoors or by a window. Move in ways that connect you to the Earth — take a barefoot walk, stretch under the sky, or practice grounding yoga poses like Tree or Warrior.

Today I nourish my body with:

Today I move with intention through:

"The Earth and I are one."

EVENING GRATITUDE

A moment I felt connected to nature today:

DAY 17—GROUND & PRESENCE
"Peace flows through me."

MORNING RITUAL

Begin your morning by sitting quietly and bringing your attention to your breath. As you inhale, imagine peace as a soft light entering through the crown of your head. As you exhale, visualize that light flowing gently through your body — clearing tension, softening muscles, calming your heart.
Repeat this for several breaths, following the natural rhythm of inhale and exhale.
Whisper slowly: "Peace moves through me with every breath I take."
(This ritual awakens a state of natural serenity, reminding you that peace is not something you seek — it's something you allow.)

_____

_____

JOURNAL REFLECTION

When do I feel most peaceful? What helps me return to that state?
What thoughts, habits, or environments disrupt my peace?
How can I let peace flow through me even in moments of challenge?
(Today's journaling helps you recognize peace not as a destination, but as an energy that moves through awareness.)

_____

_____

MEAL & MOVEMENT

Eat in a way that feels peaceful — unhurried, present, and grateful. Choose light, hydrating foods such as fruits, greens, and herbal teas. Move with flow — try tai chi, slow yoga, or a mindful walk near water to mirror the gentle movement of peace within you.

Today I nourish my body with:

_____

Today I move with intention through:

_____

"Peace is always flowing within me."

EVENING GRATITUDE
A moment when peace moved through me today:

_____

_____

DAY 18–GROUND & PRESENCE
"I find strength in stillness."

MORNING RITUAL

Start your day by taking a comfortable seat with your spine tall and your shoulders relaxed. Close your eyes and take three deep, intentional breaths.

With each inhale, feel energy rising gently through your spine. With each exhale, feel that energy root deeper into the ground beneath you.

After several breaths, place your hands over your heart and whisper:

"My power lives in peace. My strength is steady."

Sit in this stillness for one minute — noticing your pulse, your breath, your calm strength expanding.

(This ritual helps you access the quiet power within — the strength that doesn't shout, but steadies you through all things.)

MEAL & MOVEMENT

Choose grounding yet energizing meals — such as oatmeal, quinoa bowls, or lentil soup. Move mindfully — hold postures like Mountain, Tree, or Warrior with calm awareness, feeling stability as strength. Let stillness anchor your energy before and after movement.

Today I nourish my body with:

Today I move with intention through:

JOURNAL REFLECTION

When in my life have I mistaken stillness for weakness?

What happens when I pause before reacting or deciding?

How can I trust that stillness can be active and powerful?

(Today's journaling helps you reclaim your inner calm as a source of grounded power, not absence of action.)

"In stillness, I find my strength."

EVENING GRATITUDE

Stillness gave me strength today when:

DAY 19—GROUND & PRESENCE
"I am centered in gratitude."

MORNING RITUAL

Before you reach for your phone or begin your day, place one hand on your heart and take three slow, deep breaths. With each inhale, think of one thing you're grateful for — big or small. With each exhale, silently say, "Thank you."
Feel gratitude radiating from your heart like sunlight — warm, expanding, and steady.
Whisper to yourself: "Gratitude centers me in peace."
(This ritual helps you root into calm by remembering the abundance already surrounding you.)

JOURNAL REFLECTION

What am I most grateful for right now, in this moment?
How does gratitude shift my perspective when life feels uncertain?
What simple daily things do I overlook that bring me quiet joy?
(Gratitude grounds the heart in contentment — journaling today helps you see the beauty in the ordinary.)

MEAL & MOVEMENT

Eat with presence and appreciation — choose nourishing foods and silently thank each ingredient before your first bite. Move in gratitude — stretch your body slowly, acknowledging its strength, or take a mindful walk while repeating, "Thank you, life."

Today I nourish my body with:

Today I move with intention through:

"Gratitude is my anchor. I am grounded in appreciation."

EVENING GRATITUDE

Something I appreciated today that I often take for granted:

TRUEJOY-LIVING

A YEAR OF TRANSFORMATION

DAY 20-GROUND & PRESENCE
"I am calm and capable."

MORNING RITUAL

Sit comfortably and take three deep breaths, inhaling through your nose and exhaling through your mouth. On your next inhale, repeat silently: "I am calm." On your exhale, repeat: "I am capable."

Continue for several rounds until you feel your energy settle. Then, place one hand on your chest and one on your belly. Feel your breath moving between them, connecting your inner calm with your personal power.

Whisper: "I am prepared for this day, and I meet it with peace." (This ritual sets a confident tone — reminding you that calmness creates clarity, and clarity creates capability.)

MEAL & MOVEMENT

Choose balanced meals that support focus and energy — protein, whole grains, and greens. Move with intention — a morning stretch, a mindful walk, or power yoga flow, staying centered and aware of your breath throughout.

Today I nourish my body with:

Today I move with intention through:

"I am calm. I am capable. I am enough."

JOURNAL REFLECTION

What helps me stay calm when life feels uncertain?

How do I define capability — and how does calm strengthen it?

Where can I practice responding with peace instead of reacting with tension?

(Today's journaling strengthens trust — in your own steady, capable nature.)

EVENING GRATITUDE

A moment I handled calmly and confidently today:

TRUEJOY-LIVING

A YEAR OF TRANSFORMATION

DAY 21-GROUND & PRESENCE
"I honor my needs daily."

MORNING RITUAL

Begin your day with a quiet check-in. Before opening your to-do list or thinking of others, place your hand over your heart and ask yourself: "What do I truly need today — physically, emotionally, mentally, or spiritually?"
Close your eyes and take a slow, full breath as you listen for the answer. No forcing. Just noticing.
Whatever arises — rest, nourishment, quiet, connection — silently affirm: "My needs matter, and I am worthy of meeting them."
(This ritual rebalances energy, helping you lead from alignment instead of depletion.)

MEAL & MOVEMENT

Eat to nourish, not just to fuel — choose what your body truly craves for comfort and energy. Move in a way that feels like kindness — gentle yoga, restorative stretching, or rest if your body asks for stillness.

Today I nourish my body with:

_____

Today I move with intention through:

_____

JOURNAL REFLECTION

What need have I been ignoring lately, and why?
How do I feel when I give myself permission to rest, eat, or pause?
What would honoring my needs today look like in small, loving actions?
(Today's reflection helps you remember that caring for yourself is an act of strength, not selfishness.)

_____

_____

"When I care for myself, I care for my peace."

EVENING GRATITUDE

A need I honored today:

_____

_____

DAY 22-GROUND & PRESENCE
"I move with mindful intention."

MORNING RITUAL

Before beginning your day, take three slow breaths and notice how your body feels. Without judgment, simply observe — where do you feel tight, heavy, open, or energized?

Place your hands on the area that calls for attention and whisper:

"I listen to what my body needs today."

Set an intention for your movement — not to perfect, but to connect.

(This ritual helps you move from awareness instead of autopilot — bringing sacred presence to every action.)

MEAL & MOVEMENT

Choose meals that fuel you gently — fresh fruits, whole grains, and vibrant colors. Move with awareness — yoga, walking, or stretching, feeling each breath guide your motion. Let your movement be an offering of gratitude to your body.

Today I nourish my body with:

Today I move with intention through:

JOURNAL REFLECTION

How does my body feel when I move with awareness versus when I rush?

What forms of movement help me feel alive and centered?

How can I bring mindfulness into simple daily actions like walking, cleaning, or cooking?

(Today's journaling helps you realize that mindful movement isn't just physical — it's a practice of presence and love.)

> *"Each mindful step grounds me deeper in peace."*

EVENING GRATITUDE

A moment today when I moved with awareness:

DAY 23–GROUND & PRESENCE

"I nourish my body with love."

MORNING RITUAL

Before your first meal today, take a quiet moment to pause and bless your food. Look at the colors, notice the textures, and take three slow breaths before your first bite.

As you inhale, think of the earth, water, and sunlight that helped create this nourishment.

As you exhale, silently say: "May this meal fill me with peace, vitality, and love."

(This ritual transforms eating from a task into a moment of connection, gratitude, and intention.)

MEAL & MOVEMENT

Choose foods that make you feel alive — whole, colorful, and nourishing. Focus on how your body feels, not just how food tastes. Move gently after eating — take a mindful walk or stretch to help your body receive nourishment with ease.

Today I nourish my body with:

_____

Today I move with intention through:

_____

JOURNAL REFLECTION

What emotions do I often carry into my meals — gratitude, distraction, or judgment?

How does my energy shift when I eat with awareness and kindness?

What would it mean to treat every meal as an act of self-love?

(Today's reflection reconnects nourishment to self-worth — reminding you that how you feed yourself reflects how you honor yourself.)

"I am grateful for this body that sustains me."

EVENING GRATITUDE

A meal that made me feel nourished today was:

_____

_____

DAY 24-GROUND & PRESENCE
"My presence heals."

MORNING RITUAL

Begin your morning in silence. Close your eyes and bring your
awareness to your breath — slow, gentle, steady.
Visualize a soft golden light glowing in your heart center.
With each inhale, the light grows warmer and brighter.
With each exhale, it expands outward — filling your entire body
with calm, healing energy. After several breaths, whisper:
"When I am at peace, I am medicine to the world."
(This ritual reminds you that your grounded energy is a gift —
your calm presence ripples peace wherever you go.)

JOURNAL REFLECTION

How does my energy affect the spaces and people around me?
When have I noticed that my calm helped someone else feel safe?
How can I bring healing presence to my relationships — through listening,
patience, or silence?
(Your journal helps you remember that you don't have to fix others — your peace
is your contribution.)

MEAL & MOVEMENT

Eat foods that restore balance — fresh greens, citrus, herbal teas,
and warm grains. Move with gentleness and flow — try slow yoga,
mindful walking, or stretching with deep, open breaths. Let your
energy move freely, not forcefully.

Today I nourish my body with:

_____

Today I move with intention through:

_____

> *"Peace flows through me and
> around me.*

EVENING GRATITUDE

A moment I brought peace to another today was:

_____

_____

DAY 25-GROUND & PRESENCE

"I am grounded in trust."

MORNING RITUAL

Begin your morning with both feet firmly on the floor. Close
your eyes, inhale deeply, and imagine drawing strength up from
the earth through your feet. As you exhale, feel yourself
releasing doubt and control into the ground beneath you.
Say softly: "I trust that everything is unfolding as it should."
"I am safe in the timing of my life."
Take one more grounding breath, standing tall in quiet
confidence.
(This ritual invites peace through surrender — helping you
remember that life supports you even when you can't see how.)

_____

_____

JOURNAL REFLECTION

Where in my life am I trying to control the outcome?
What would it feel like to release that and trust in timing?
How has trust led me to peace or unexpected blessings in the
past?
(Today's journaling deepens faith — not as blind optimism, but as
calm surrender to the rhythm of life.)

_____

_____

MEAL & MOVEMENT

Choose meals that symbolize balance and patience — like slow-
cooked foods, roasted vegetables, or herbal teas. Move with grace
and steadiness — try a slow-flow yoga practice or an intentional
walk, matching each step to your breath.

Today I nourish my body with:

_____

Today I move with intention through:

_____

"I am held. I am guided. I am grounded in trust."

EVENING GRATITUDE

A moment today when I trusted instead of controlling:

_____

_____

DAY 26-GROUND & PRESENCE
"Peace lives within me."

MORNING RITUAL

Before starting your day, place both hands over your heart.
Close your eyes and breathe in through your nose, out through your mouth.
With each inhale, imagine drawing peace into your body.
With each exhale, feel that peace expand and fill every cell.
Repeat slowly: "Peace is not outside me — it lives within."
Stay here for a few breaths, resting in that truth.
Notice how your body softens as you remember: you are peace.
(This ritual grounds you in self-trust — reminding you that peace isn't found, it's felt.)

MEAL & MOVEMENT

Choose foods that bring ease and comfort — herbal teas, soups, or lightly seasoned grains. Move with serenity — try gentle yoga, mindful stretching, or still meditation. Let each action today feel like an act of peace.

Today I nourish my body with:

_____

Today I move with intention through:

_____

JOURNAL REFLECTION

When was the last time I truly felt peaceful — what created that state?
What thoughts or habits block me from accessing my inner peace?
How can I return to my inner calm more often throughout my day?
(Today's journaling reveals that peace is not a destination — it's the quiet truth beneath every breath.)

"Peace is my nature. I am whole. I am calm. I am free."

EVENING GRATITUDE

A peaceful moment I experienced today:

_____

DAY 27–GROUND & PRESENCE
"I am rooted in gratitude and grace."

MORNING RITUAL

Begin your day with a gentle stretch or by standing tall
with your feet grounded. Close your eyes and take three
slow breaths — in through your nose, out through your
mouth. As you inhale, repeat silently: "I am grateful." As
you exhale, whisper: "I give myself grace."

Visualize roots of golden light extending from your feet
deep into the earth — steady, soft, and full of life. Feel
yourself supported, loved, and enough exactly as you are.
(This ritual unites appreciation and self-acceptance —
creating emotional balance and spiritual calm.)

JOURNAL REFLECTION

Where can I offer myself more grace in this season of life?
How does gratitude help me soften and open to joy?
What simple things today remind me of the beauty of being alive?
(Today's reflection helps you blend gratitude with gentleness — a
reminder that grace is a form of love.)

MEAL & MOVEMENT

Nourish yourself with foods that bring comfort and joy —
perhaps something warm or made with care. Move slowly
and gently — flow with awareness, dance freely, or take a
mindful walk while repeating, "Thank you. I forgive. I
allow."

Today I nourish my body with:

Today I move with intention through:

"Gratitude anchors me. Grace restores me. I am rooted in both."

EVENING GRATITUDE

A moment of grace I gave myself today:

DAY 28-GROUND & PRESENCE
"I release what I cannot control."

MORNING RITUAL

Sit comfortably, close your eyes, and take a deep
breath in through your nose. As you exhale, imagine
letting go of one thought, worry, or expectation that's
been weighing on you. Place your hands open on your
lap, palms facing upward — a symbol of surrender and
faith.
 Whisper softly: "I trust the flow of life."
"I let go of what's not mine to carry."
Feel the tension leave your body as you breathe.
(This ritual reminds you that peace begins the moment
you stop fighting what you can't change.)

_____

_____

MEAL & MOVEMENT

Choose simple, soothing meals today — warm soups,
teas, or steamed vegetables that feel cleansing. Move to
release — try gentle twists, restorative yoga, or slow
walking. Let your body exhale what your heart no longer
needs to hold.

Today I nourish my body with:

_____

Today I move with intention through:

_____

JOURNAL REFLECTION

What am I holding onto that is no longer serving me?
How might life feel if I truly released control?
What would trust look like in this situation?
(Journaling today helps you find freedom through surrender —
trusting that letting go is not losing, but opening.)

_____

_____

*"I am safe to let go. I am guided.
I am free."*

EVENING GRATITUDE

Something I chose to release today:

_____

_____

DAY 29–GROUND & PRESENCE
"I am fully present in this moment."

MORNING RITUAL

When you wake, before reaching for your phone or moving from bed, take three mindful breaths. With each inhale, silently say: "I am here."
With each exhale: "Now."
Sit up slowly, stretch, and notice the feeling of your body waking -
the air, the light, the sounds around you.
For one full minute, do nothing but be in this exact moment.
Whisper: "This moment is enough."
(This ritual helps you meet the day with awareness and peace — grounding your energy in presence rather than anticipation.)

MEAL & MOVEMENT

Eat with full attention — no distractions, no screens, just you and your meal. Savor every flavor and texture. Move in mindfulness — walk, stretch, or breathe with awareness of every motion, letting your senses anchor you to the now.

Today I nourish my body with:

_____

Today I move with intention through:

_____

JOURNAL REFLECTION

What am I holding onto that is no longer serving me?
How might life feel if I truly released control?
What would trust look like in this situation?
(Journaling today helps you find freedom through surrender — trusting that letting go is not losing, but opening.)

_____

_____

"I am here. I am now. I am whole."

EVENING GRATITUDE
A moment today when I felt completely present:

_____

_____

DAY 30-GROUND & PRESENCE
"I am grounded in peace and purpose."

MORNING RITUAL

Begin the morning by lighting a candle or taking three intentional breaths.
As you inhale, think: "Peace fills me." As you exhale, whisper: "Purpose guides me."
Reflect for a moment on your journey through the past 30 days.
What has shifted in your heart? What do you now understand about your strength, your body, your presence?
Take one more deep, grounding breath and affirm:
"I am rooted in peace. I am guided by purpose. I am ready for what's next."
(This ritual seals your growth — a calm acknowledgment of how far you've come and the energy you now embody.)

JOURNAL REFLECTION

What lessons from these 30 days feel most alive in me?
How has grounding changed the way I approach daily life?
What does peace mean to me now? What does purpose feel like in my body?
(Today's journaling honors integration — a time to recognize growth before beginning the next evolution of your transformation.)

MEAL & MOVEMENT

Choose a meal that feels celebratory yet nourishing — something colorful, whole, and made with intention. Move in gratitude — walk outdoors, stretch with music, or flow through yoga, honoring how your body supports you each day.

Today I nourish my body with:

Today I move with intention through:

"I am grounded. I am present. I am becoming."

EVENING GRATITUDE
One shift I'm most grateful for this month:

DAY 31-AWAKEN & EXPANSION
"I am grounded in peace and purpose."

MORNING RITUAL

Before you begin your day, take three deep breaths and imagine a soft light rising within you — like the first glow of dawn.
With each inhale, invite openness and curiosity.
With each exhale, release old patterns or expectations that feel heavy.
Whisper gently: I welcome what's new. I am open to possibility."
Spend one minute visualizing yourself stepping into a new chapter — calm, capable, and ready to grow.
(This ritual awakens creative energy and reminds you that every morning is a new beginning.)

JOURNAL REFLECTION

What feels ready to awaken in me right now?
What dreams or ideas have been quietly waiting for my attention?
How can I approach today with curiosity instead of control?
(Today's reflection opens the mind to expansion — reminding you that awakening happens when you allow life to surprise you.)

MEAL & MOVEMENT

Eat foods that awaken your senses — fresh fruits, vibrant greens, or citrus-infused water. Move to energize — a morning stretch, a brisk walk, or dance freely to uplifting music. Let your movement feel like renewal.

Today I nourish my body with:

Today I move with intention through:

"Each day I awaken more fully to myself."

EVENING GRATITUDE

A new possibility or perspective I noticed today:

DAY 32-AWAKEN & EXPANSION
"I embrace curiosity and growth."

MORNING RITUAL

Start your morning by taking a deep breath and saying aloud:
"Today, I choose curiosity over fear."
As you move through your morning routine — brushing your
teeth, stretching, sipping tea — do each task with fresh eyes.
Notice something new: the light, the scent, the sounds.
Bring childlike wonder to ordinary moments.
(This ritual trains your mind to awaken through awareness —
finding joy in what's already here.)

MEAL & MOVEMENT

Try something new — a fresh recipe, a new spice, or a
meal you've never made before. Move differently —
take a new route on your walk, try a new yoga flow, or
simply let your body move intuitively. Curiosity invites
energy and joy.

Today I nourish my body with:

_____

Today I move with intention through:

_____

JOURNAL REFLECTION

Where in my life am I being invited to grow?
What am I curious about but have hesitated to explore?
How does it feel to view challenges as opportunities for learning?
(Curiosity transforms fear into freedom — journaling today helps you see
possibility where doubt once lived.)

*"I am open, curious, and growing
every day."*

EVENING GRATITUDE

Something new I tried or noticed today:

_____

DAY 33-AWAKEN & EXPANSION
"I listen to my inner guidance."

MORNING RITUAL

Find a quiet space and take three slow breaths. Place one hand over your heart and the other on your belly.
As you inhale, say silently: "I open to receive."
As you exhale: "I trust what I hear."
Close your eyes and ask your higher self:
"What do I need to know or remember today?"
Don't force an answer — just listen. Notice the first feeling, word, or image that arises. Carry it with you as your quiet intention for the day.
(This ritual builds trust between your mind and your intuition — reconnecting you to inner wisdom.)

JOURNAL REFLECTION

When was the last time I listened to my intuition — and what happened?
What signs or sensations tell me that my inner voice is speaking?
Where in my life am I being asked to trust my inner knowing more deeply?
(Today's reflection strengthens self-trust — reminding you that wisdom already lives within you.)

MEAL & MOVEMENT

Eat intuitively — choose what feels nourishing rather than what you "should" eat. Move with awareness — yoga, stretching, or walking in silence. Let your body lead and your mind follow.

Today I nourish my body with:

_____

Today I move with intention through:

_____

"My intuition is clear, kind, and always guiding me toward my highest good."

EVENING GRATITUDE

A moment when I followed my intuition today:

_____

_____

DAY 34-AWAKEN & EXPANSION
"I awaken my creative energy."

MORNING RITUAL

Begin your morning by taking three deep breaths and rolling your shoulders back to open your heart space. Visualize a warm golden light glowing in your lower belly — the center of your creative power. With each breath, imagine that light growing brighter, spreading through your chest and fingertips.
Say softly: "Creative energy flows freely through me."
Spend one minute noticing what ideas, images, or feelings arise — no judgment, just flow.
(This ritual reconnects you to your natural state of creation — open, curious, and inspired.)

JOURNAL REFLECTION

What does creativity mean to me beyond art — how do I create in daily life?
Where might I be blocking my creative flow with fear or overthinking?
What simple action could I take today to express my authentic self?
(Creativity is the soul in motion — journaling helps you remember that expression itself is healing.)

MEAL & MOVEMENT

Choose vibrant, colorful foods today — fruits, herbs, and spices that awaken your senses. Move playfully — dance, flow, or stretch with music. Let your body express freedom and joy.

Today I nourish my body with:

Today I move with intention through:

"I am a vessel of creation. Inspiration flows through me with ease."

EVENING GRATITUDE

A moment I felt inspired or creative today:

TRUEJOY-LIVING
A YEAR OF TRANSFORMATION

DAY 35–AWAKEN & EXPANSION
"I welcome expansion and flow."

MORNING RITUAL

Begin your day with three deep breaths.
As you inhale, feel your chest and ribs expand.
As you exhale, release any tightness or resistance.
Stretch your arms wide and say aloud:
"I am open to growth. I flow with life."
Visualize yourself standing in a river of golden light —
calm yet ever-moving.
You don't need to control it. You simply allow it to carry
you gently forward.
(This ritual reminds you that growth doesn't require force
— only openness and trust.)

MEAL & MOVEMENT

Eat meals that feel light yet energizing — greens,
citrus, grains, and herbal teas. Move like water —
through flowing yoga, dancing, or intuitive
stretching. Let your breath and movement feel
spacious, effortless, and alive.

Today I nourish my body with:

_____

Today I move with intention through:

_____

JOURNAL REFLECTION

Where in my life am I being invited to expand?
What am I resisting that might actually be helping me grow?
How can I allow life to flow through me instead of trying to control it?
(Today's journaling invites surrender into expansion — trusting that ease and
growth can exist together.)

_____

_____

*"I am open. I am expanding.
I am in flow with life."*

EVENING GRATITUDE

A moment I allowed flow instead of control today:

_____

_____

TRUEJOY-LIVING

A YEAR OF TRANSFORMATION

DAY 36—AWAKEN & EXPANSION

"I am awake to life's magic."

MORNING RITUAL

Begin your day with your eyes closed and take a slow, intentional breath.
As you inhale, whisper: "I open my eyes to wonder."
As you exhale, say: "Magic is all around me."
Now open your eyes slowly and notice — the colors, the light, the sounds of life waking up.
Spend one minute simply seeing the world as if for the first time.
Let this truth settle in your heart: Life's magic reveals itself to those who are willing to notice.
(This ritual awakens awe — helping you remember that joy lives in awareness, not achievement.)

JOURNAL REFLECTION

What moments recently have felt magical or synchronistic?
When I slow down and notice, what beauty or blessings reveal themselves?
How can I keep my heart open to everyday miracles?
(Today's reflection helps you see that magic isn't rare — it's revealed through mindful presence and gratitude.)

MEAL & MOVEMENT

Choose meals that delight your senses — fresh fruit, bright herbs, or something beautifully plated. Move with joy — dance while cooking, stretch in sunlight, or walk with gratitude for the miracle of being alive.

Today I nourish my body with:

Today I move with intention through:

"I am awake, alive, and guided by life's magic."

EVENING GRATITUDE

A magical or beautiful moment I experienced today:

DAY 37-AWAKEN & EXPANSION

"I am expanding beyond fear."

MORNING RITUAL

Take three deep breaths, feeling your feet rooted firmly on the ground.
As you inhale, imagine drawing in courage and light.
As you exhale, visualize fear leaving your body as mist dissolving into the air.
Now place your hand on your heart and whisper:
"I see my fear. I thank it for trying to protect me."
"And now, I choose to grow beyond it."
Sit for a few quiet breaths, letting gratitude soften what feels tense.
(This ritual teaches that fear isn't the enemy — it's a messenger guiding you toward freedom.)

MEAL & MOVEMENT

Choose foods that bring grounded energy and warmth — roasted root vegetables, whole grains, or herbal teas. Move with empowerment — strong, steady yoga poses, mindful walking, or breath-led flow to build confidence through motion.

Today I nourish my body with:

_____

Today I move with intention through:

_____

JOURNAL REFLECTION

What fear is currently asking for my attention — and what truth lives beneath it?
How does my body feel when fear arises, and what helps me move through it?
What would I do today if I trusted myself fully?
(Today's journaling helps transform fear into fuel — an invitation to step forward with courage and clarity.)

_____

_____

"I am safe to grow. I am brave enough to expand."

EVENING GRATITUDE

A fear I faced or softened today:

_____

_____

DAY 38–AWAKEN & EXPANSION
"I awaken to my inner light."

MORNING RITUAL

Sit quietly and close your eyes. Take a slow, deep breath and bring your awareness to your heart center. Visualize a soft golden light glowing there — small but steady. With every inhale, see that light grow brighter, expanding through your chest and body. With every exhale, let it radiate outward — filling your space with warmth and calm.

Whisper softly: "My light shines naturally. I no longer dim to fit in."

Take one more deep breath and allow that light to remind you — you are already enough.

(This ritual connects you to your divine essence — the quiet power that lives within you at all times.)

_____

_____

JOURNAL REFLECTION

When do I feel most connected to my inner light?
What thoughts or patterns tend to dim that light?
How can I share my light today — through kindness, honesty, or creativity?
(Journaling today helps you remember that your light doesn't compete — it illuminates.)

_____

_____

MEAL & MOVEMENT

Eat foods that energize and uplift — bright fruits, nourishing grains, and water infused with lemon or herbs. Move with grace — a morning stretch in sunlight, dance to your favorite song, or flow freely to feel your inner radiance expand.

Today I nourish my body with:

_____

Today I move with intention through:

_____

> *"My light is steady, sacred, and always within me."*

EVENING GRATITUDE

A moment I felt my light shine today:

_____

_____

DAY 39-AWAKEN & EXPANSION

"I see possibility everywhere."

MORNING RITUAL

Say aloud:
"I am open to all the possibilities this day brings."
As you get ready for your morning, pause once or twice to notice the small wonders around you — the sunlight, the scent of coffee, the sound of life stirring.
Let your awareness remind you: possibility is always present.
Close with a grounding breath and whisper:
"I trust that new paths are unfolding for me now."
(This ritual trains your awareness toward abundance — seeing opportunity and alignment where fear once saw limitation.)

JOURNAL REFLECTION

Where in my life have I been limiting what's possible for me?
What would it look like to choose faith over fear in that area?
How can I practice seeing opportunity instead of obstacles today?
(Today's reflection opens the inner vision — awakening your ability to spot blessings and invitations for growth everywhere.)

MEAL & MOVEMENT

Try something new today — a recipe, a flavor, or a way of moving. Eat with openness to new tastes and experiences. Move expansively — arms wide, chest open, shoulders relaxed — embodying receptivity to life's possibilities.

Today I nourish my body with:

Today I move with intention through:

"I live in a world full of possibility."

EVENING GRATITUDE

A new possibility or insight I noticed today:

DAY 40-AWAKEN & EXPANSION
"I trust my path."

MORNING RITUAL

Begin your morning by sitting quietly with your eyes closed and both feet planted firmly on the floor.
Place your hands on your heart and take three deep, steady breaths.
On each inhale, say silently: "I am guided."
On each exhale: "I trust the path unfolding for me."
Visualize yourself walking a path of golden light stretching ahead — not fully visible, but glowing with calm certainty.
You don't need to see the destination. You only need to trust each step.
(This ritual brings peace to uncertainty, anchoring your spirit in divine timing and inner guidance.)

_____

_____

JOURNAL REFLECTION

Where in my life am I being asked to trust more deeply?
What fears or doubts make me question my direction?
How can I release the need to know "how" and rest in "I am guided"?
(Today's reflection transforms uncertainty into faith — reminding you that trust builds the bridge before it's visible.)

_____

_____

MEAL & MOVEMENT

Choose comforting, grounding foods — oats, rice, or roasted vegetables. Move in flow — yoga, slow walking, or breathwork. Let each movement mirror trust: no rush, no resistance, only rhythm and ease.

Today I nourish my body with:

_____

Today I move with intention through:

_____

"My steps are guided. My path is sacred. I trust where I am."

EVENING GRATITUDE

A moment today when I trusted instead of worrying:

_____

_____

DAY 41-AWAKEN & EXPANSION
"I am open to divine guidance."

MORNING RITUAL

Start your morning in quiet reflection. Take three slow, deep breaths, inhaling peace and exhaling resistance. Place your hand over your heart and whisper:

"I am open to receive guidance today."

Sit in stillness for a minute or two, noticing any sensations, thoughts, or feelings that arise.

Then say softly:

"I trust that I am always guided, protected, and supported."

Carry this awareness into your day — open eyes, open heart, open mind.

(This ritual helps you align your energy with guidance — not by forcing answers, but by allowing them to appear in perfect time.)

JOURNAL REFLECTION

How does divine guidance show up for me — through intuition, people, signs, or synchronicities?

Where have I ignored guidance in the past, and what did I learn?

How can I stay open to receive messages from life with trust and calm?

(Today's reflection strengthens faith in your unseen support — helping you listen deeply to the whispers of the universe.)

MEAL & MOVEMENT

Eat with gratitude for life's provision — simple, fresh meals that nourish your body and keep you light. Move mindfully — walking, yoga, or breathwork — and ask for clarity as you move, letting inspiration arrive through stillness or motion.

Today I nourish my body with:

Today I move with intention through:

"I am guided by love. I am led by light."

EVENING GRATITUDE

A moment I felt guided or supported today:

DAY 42-AWAKEN & EXPANSION

"My intentions shape my reality."

MORNING RITUAL

Take a few quiet breaths and bring your awareness into your heart.
Ask yourself: "How do I want to feel today?"
Once you have your answer, write down one clear, loving intention for the day — something that uplifts you and others.
Example: "Today, I move with calm confidence." or "Today, I choose joy over hurry." Repeat your intention aloud and take three slow breaths as if you're breathing life into it.
 Visualize yourself living that intention throughout the day with ease.
(This ritual aligns your thoughts, energy, and actions — reminding you that life flows in the direction of your focus.)

_____

_____

JOURNAL REFLECTION

What intentions currently guide my actions?
Are they aligned with my values and how I want to feel?
How can I bring more purpose and awareness to simple daily choices?
(Today's reflection transforms routine into ritual — showing how every thought and action becomes part of conscious creation.)

_____

_____

MEAL & MOVEMENT

Eat intentionally — prepare your meal with mindfulness, blessing your food with gratitude. Choose clean, balanced ingredients that support focus and energy. Move with purpose — walk, stretch, or flow while repeating your intention silently.

Today I nourish my body with:

_____

Today I move with intention through:

_____

"I live intentionally. I create consciously. I am aligned with my purpose.

EVENING GRATITUDE

The intention I set today was:

_____

_____

DAY 43-AWAKEN & EXPANSION
"I am guided by purpose, not pressure."

MORNING RITUAL

Begin your morning with three grounding breaths.
With your eyes closed, place one hand on your heart and whisper:
"Today, I move with purpose, not push."
Visualize your day flowing like a river — calm, steady, unforced.
You still move forward, but with grace instead of strain.
Take one more deep breath and allow peace to replace pressure.
(This ritual reminds you that true productivity comes from presence — not from force.)

JOURNAL REFLECTION

Where in my life am I acting from pressure rather than purpose?
How does it feel when I work or create from inspiration instead of urgency?
What would living guided by purpose look like in my daily rhythm?
(Today's reflection replaces striving with flow — helping you recognize that peace and progress can coexist.)

MEAL & MOVEMENT

Eat slowly and intentionally — choose meals that fuel sustainable energy, not just quick bursts. Move gently but purposefully — yoga, stretching, or walking with awareness of breath and gratitude. Let your body model balanced effort and ease.

Today I nourish my body with:

_____

Today I move with intention through:

_____

"I am aligned, not rushed. I move at the speed of purpose."

EVENING GRATITUDE

A moment I followed purpose over pressure today:

_____

DAY 44-AWAKEN & EXPANSION

"My intuition is my inner compass."

MORNING RITUAL

Find a calm space and sit comfortably. Close your eyes and take three slow, grounding breaths. Place your hands on your heart and whisper:
"I am listening."
Ask silently: "What would bring me peace and alignment today?"
Don't rush to answer — instead, notice what arises naturally: a word, an image, a feeling, a quiet knowing. Write it down or hold it in your heart as your guiding message for the day.
(This ritual helps strengthen your trust in inner guidance — the voice that always knows your next right step.)

MEAL & MOVEMENT

Eat intuitively — pause before your meal and ask your body what it needs: grounding, freshness, warmth, or lightness. Move with inner awareness — yoga, walking, or stretching guided by how your body feels, not by rules or routine.

Today I nourish my body with:

_____

Today I move with intention through:

_____

JOURNAL REFLECTION

When have I followed my intuition and felt deeply aligned?
What signals does my intuition use — sensations, emotions, synchronicities?
Where in my life am I being invited to trust my inner knowing more fully?
(Journaling today helps you recognize intuition as a relationship — one that grows stronger with attention and trust.)

_____

_____

"I honor the quiet voice within. It always leads me home."

EVENING GRATITUDE

A moment when I listened to my intuition today:

_____

_____

DAY 45-AWAKEN & EXPANSION

"I am expanding in awareness and truth."

MORNING RITUAL

Find stillness. Sit comfortably, spine tall, shoulders relaxed. Take three deep breaths, in through your nose and out through your mouth.

With each inhale, imagine light filling your mind and heart.

With each exhale, release outdated thoughts, stories, or labels that no longer serve you. Place your hands over your heart and whisper:

"I am open to seeing truth clearly."

Sit for a few moments, simply observing your thoughts — not judging, not attaching, just noticing. Awareness itself is awakening.

(This ritual expands consciousness — creating space for truth, perspective, and inner peace to arise.)

JOURNAL REFLECTION

What truths am I awakening to in my life right now?

Which beliefs, habits, or fears no longer align with who I'm becoming?

What feels lighter, freer, or more authentic when I let go of illusion or expectation?

(Journaling today helps you replace old narratives with clear, compassionate awareness — the essence of awakening.)

MEAL & MOVEMENT

Choose light, cleansing foods — leafy greens, herbal teas, or lemon water to support clarity. Move with intention — slow flow yoga, deep breathing, or open-arm stretches that create physical and energetic space for new insight.

Today I nourish my body with:

_____

Today I move with intention through:

_____

"Awareness is my light. Truth is my freedom."

EVENING GRATITUDE

A truth that became clearer to me today:

_____

_____

DAY 46–AWAKEN & EXPANSION
"Joy flows naturally when I am in alignment."

MORNING RITUAL
Begin the morning by taking three slow breaths — in through your nose, out through your mouth. As you inhale, imagine your breath filling you with light.

As you exhale, release anything that feels forced, rushed, or disconnected.

Place your hand on your heart and whisper: "I choose alignment over effort."

"Joy is the rhythm of my truth."

Sit for one quiet minute and allow a smile — even a small one — to rise naturally. Feel that joy as a vibration in your body, soft but powerful.

(This ritual awakens lightness and flow, reminding you that joy appears when you move in sync with your authentic self.)

_____

_____

JOURNAL REFLECTION
When do I feel most in alignment with myself?

What activities or choices naturally bring me joy and energy?

How can I create more space for joy to flow freely in my daily life?

(Today's reflection helps you understand that joy is a compass — it points you toward truth, peace, and alignment.)

_____

_____

MEAL & MOVEMENT
Eat meals that feel vibrant and energizing — bright vegetables, colorful fruits, or a meal you truly enjoy. Move in ways that spark joy — dance, flow yoga, or a walk while listening to uplifting music. Let movement be celebration, not obligation.

Today I nourish my body with:

_____

Today I move with intention through:

_____

"Joy is my nature. Alignment is my way."

EVENING GRATITUDE
A moment joy flowed naturally today:

_____

_____

DAY 47—AWAKEN & EXPANSION

"I expand through love."

MORNING RITUAL

Sit quietly and take three slow breaths. As you inhale, visualize light entering your heart — warm, radiant, golden. As you exhale, imagine that light expanding outward — through your chest, your body, your aura, your space.

Whisper softly: "I open my heart to love." "I give and receive with ease."

Now bring to mind someone, something, or even a moment that fills you with gratitude or tenderness. Feel that love grow within you until it overflows.

That energy — unconditional, peaceful, and kind — is the essence of expansion.

(This ritual reminds you that love is your truest power — it transforms everything it touches.)

JOURNAL REFLECTION

How does love move through me — toward myself, others, and life?

Where can I replace judgment with compassion?

How would it feel to make every choice today from love instead of fear?

(Journaling today opens the heart wider — showing how love naturally expands awareness, purpose, and peace.)

MEAL & MOVEMENT

Eat with love and presence — choose meals that feel nourishing and heartwarming, maybe something homemade or shared. Move with grace — flowing stretches, gentle yoga, or dancing with an open chest. Let love infuse your every movement.

Today I nourish my body with:

Today I move with intention through:

"Love flows through me endlessly. I expand with grace."

EVENING GRATITUDE

A moment love guided me today:

TRUEJOY-LIVING

A YEAR OF TRANSFORMATION

DAY 48-AWAKEN & EXPANSION
"I awaken with courage and clarity."

MORNING RITUAL

Sit in stillness and take a slow, deep breath. As you inhale, say silently: "I breathe in courage." As you exhale: "I release doubt." Place one hand on your heart and one on your solar plexus (just above the navel). Visualize a golden light connecting the two — your love and your power uniting in balance.

Whisper softly: "I see clearly. I move bravely."

Let this energy fill your body — calm, confident, and centered.

Then open your eyes and take one inspired action that aligns with your truth today.

(This ritual strengthens clarity through courage — reminding you that confidence grows from connection, not control.)

MEAL & MOVEMENT

Choose energizing meals — whole grains, leafy greens, and bright citrus to support focus. Move with power and precision — grounding poses, brisk walking, or breath-led strength exercises that remind you of your steadiness.

Today I nourish my body with:

Today I move with intention through:

JOURNAL REFLECTION

What does courage mean to me right now — and where is it most needed?

What truths or desires are becoming clearer as I awaken?

How can I take one small, brave step toward alignment today?

(Today's reflection helps you turn awareness into action — bringing clarity from the mind into the heart, and from the heart into movement.)

"I see clearly. I trust deeply. I walk with courage and grace."

EVENING GRATITUDE

A moment I acted with courage today:

DAY 49-AWAKEN & EXPANSION

"I am becoming, and that is beautiful."

MORNING RITUAL

Sit comfortably with one hand over your heart.
Take a slow breath in through your nose and release through your mouth.
As you breathe, imagine a soft light surrounding you — not yet complete, but always expanding.
Whisper gently:
"I honor where I am. I trust where I'm going."
Spend a minute noticing how far you've come — not what's left to do.
Smile softly at your own evolution.
(This ritual invites peace with progress — a reminder that growth is a journey, not a finish line.)

MEAL & MOVEMENT

Choose meals that reflect balance and nourishment — foods that make you feel whole, like bowls with grains, greens, and color. Move gracefully — stretching, slow flow yoga, or a mindful walk, matching your pace to your breath. Let each motion symbolize your unfolding.

Today I nourish my body with:

_____

Today I move with intention through:

_____

JOURNAL REFLECTION

How have I changed in the last few weeks or months?
What old layers or beliefs am I shedding as I grow?
Can I appreciate this stage of becoming instead of rushing the outcome?
(Today's reflection helps you fall in love with the process — seeing beauty in evolution and compassion in progress.)

_____

_____

"I am a masterpiece in motion. Becoming is my beauty."

EVENING GRATITUDE

Something I noticed about my growth today:

_____

_____

TRUEJOY-LIVING

A YEAR OF TRANSFORMATION

DAY 50 – AWAKEN & EXPANSION
"I create balance in all that I do."

MORNING RITUAL

Begin the morning in stillness.
Close your eyes and imagine a soft, golden scale inside your chest — perfectly balanced between giving and receiving, effort and rest, doing and being.
Take three deep breaths and repeat softly:
"I am centered. I am steady. I am in harmony."
As you move through your morning, pause once to check in with yourself — "Am I grounded or scattered?" Adjust your pace, your breath, or your focus to bring yourself back to balance.
(This ritual helps you move through the day with calm rhythm — responsive, not reactive.)

JOURNAL REFLECTION

Where do I feel out of balance — physically, emotionally, or mentally?
What small actions help restore harmony in my day?
How can I create more space for rest without guilt and productivity without pressure?
(Today's reflection guides you toward sustainable energy — reminding you that balance is a living practice, not a perfect state.)

MEAL & MOVEMENT

Eat for harmony — choose meals with both nourishment and lightness: greens with grains, warm foods balanced by freshness. Move to restore equilibrium — yoga, Pilates, or slow walking to align breath and body. Balance strength with surrender

Today I nourish my body with:

_____

Today I move with intention through:

_____

"I live in balance. I flow in harmony. I rest in peace."

EVENING GRATITUDE

A moment I felt balanced and peaceful today:

_____

_____

DAY 51—AWAKEN & EXPANSION

"I am open to infinite possibility."

MORNING RITUAL

Begin your day by standing tall, shoulders relaxed, feet grounded. Take a deep breath and stretch your arms open wide. As you inhale, imagine you're drawing in light from all around — endless potential filling your lungs.

As you exhale, whisper: "I am open to receive."

Take a few quiet moments to visualize your life expanding — not through effort, but through openness. See opportunities, joy, and alignment flowing toward you like sunlight.

(This ritual opens your energy field to possibility — reminding you that miracles move through those who stay open.)

JOURNAL REFLECTION

Where have I been limiting my potential or possibilities?

What would life look like if I fully trusted that anything is possible?

How can I create space — mentally, emotionally, or physically — for new opportunities to flow in?

(Today's reflection helps you release small thinking and align with the energy of abundance, expansion, and trust.)

MEAL & MOVEMENT

Eat foods that feel expansive and fresh — colorful fruits, greens, seeds, and plenty of water. Move freely — dance, flow, or stretch with arms wide and heart open. Let movement mirror expansion: big, bright, unrestrained.

Today I nourish my body with:

_____

Today I move with intention through:

_____

> "The universe is vast, and so am I."
> "I am open to all that is meant for me."

EVENING GRATITUDE

A new possibility or insight I became aware of today:

_____

_____

_____

DAY 52-AWAKEN & EXPANSION

"I am in alignment with the universe."

MORNING RITUAL

Find a quiet space and sit comfortably. Take three deep breaths — inhaling through your nose, exhaling slowly through your mouth. As you inhale, whisper: "I align with peace." As you exhale: "I align with flow."

Now visualize yourself standing beneath a golden stream of light — the loving energy of the universe pouring down through you.

Feel this light connecting you to everything: the earth, the stars, the hearts of others. Whisper softly:

"I am connected. I am supported. I am in perfect alignment."

(This ritual helps you remember you're never separate — your life is a conversation with the universe, always unfolding in harmony.)

MEAL & MOVEMENT

Eat in harmony with nature — fresh, seasonal foods and plenty of water. Move with flow — tai chi, yoga, or a mindful walk in nature. Focus on moving with your breath, not against it — like a dance with life itself.

Today I nourish my body with:

_____

Today I move with intention through:

_____

JOURNAL REFLECTION

How does alignment feel in my body and energy?

What signs or synchronicities have shown me I'm on the right path?

Where in my life do I feel resistance, and how can I return to flow?

(Today's reflection helps you see that alignment isn't about perfection — it's about presence, trust, and movement in harmony with life.)

_____

_____

"I am part of the great unfolding. The universe and I move as one."

EVENING GRATITUDE

A moment today when I felt in flow or alignment:

_____

_____

DAY 53–AWAKEN & EXPANSION
"I trust the flow of my life."

MORNING RITUAL

Sit quietly and take three deep, cleansing breaths. As you inhale, imagine a wave of calm energy washing over you. As you exhale, feel yourself releasing the need to control, push, or rush.

Now picture yourself floating in a gentle current of light — supported, guided, and safe. Whisper softly: "I release resistance. I flow with ease."

Take one more deep breath and allow that image of effortless movement to stay with you throughout the day.

(This ritual reminds you that when you surrender to flow, you align with the natural rhythm of abundance and peace.)

JOURNAL REFLECTION

Where in my life am I trying to force outcomes instead of trusting flow?

What happens when I relax into the natural rhythm of things?

How does it feel to trust timing instead of trying to control it?

(Today's reflection transforms surrender into strength — reminding you that flow leads exactly where you're meant to go.)

MEAL & MOVEMENT

Choose meals that feel light yet sustaining — think warm grains, fruit, and tea. Move fluidly — slow yoga, swimming, or intuitive stretching. Let your body mimic water: adaptable, graceful, and free.

Today I nourish my body with:

_____

Today I move with intention through:

_____

"I am one with the flow. I am carried by grace."

EVENING GRATITUDE

A moment today when I felt in flow:

_____

_____

DAY 54–AWAKEN & EXPANSION
"I am ready to live my highest potential."

MORNING RITUAL

Begin your morning by placing your hand on your heart and taking three slow, intentional breaths. As you inhale, whisper: "I rise in my truth." As you exhale: "I release all limits."

Now, visualize your best, most radiant self — standing tall, peaceful, and confident. See this version of you moving through the day with clarity, compassion, and purpose.

Whisper softly: "I am becoming all that I am meant to be."

(This ritual calls forth your inner power and reminds you that your potential already lives within — awakening simply reveals it.)

JOURNAL REFLECTION

What does my "highest potential" look and feel like — emotionally, spiritually, physically?

What habits, thoughts, or fears hold me back from fully stepping into that version of myself?

What one aligned action can I take today to embody my highest self?

(Today's reflection bridges possibility and embodiment — turning vision into lived reality.)

MEAL & MOVEMENT

Eat meals that feel empowering — vibrant, whole, and full of life energy (like greens, quinoa, citrus, or herbal teas). Move with confidence — strong yoga poses, a morning walk, or any movement that makes you feel powerful and alive.

Today I nourish my body with:

Today I move with intention through:

"I am ready. I am capable. I am becoming my fullest expression."

EVENING GRATITUDE

A moment I embodied my highest potential today:

DAY 55—AWAKEN & EXPANSION
"Peace and trust guide my every step."

MORNING RITUAL

Begin your day in silence. Take a deep breath in through your nose, feeling your lungs expand. Exhale slowly through your mouth, releasing any tension or lingering thoughts. Repeat this three times. Now place both hands over your heart and whisper: "I trust life's timing. I move in peace."

Visualize your heart radiating calm — a steady rhythm, unbothered by the world around it.

Carry that stillness with you into your morning.

(This ritual helps you embody peaceful expansion — teaching that trust, not tension, keeps your energy aligned with flow.)

JOURNAL REFLECTION

What does peace feel like in my body and energy?

Where in my life can I replace effort with trust?

How would it feel to let go of control and allow life to unfold naturally?

(Today's reflection anchors you back into faith and softness — the space where true alignment thrives.)

MEAL & MOVEMENT

Eat simple, grounding meals — soups, steamed vegetables, or oatmeal. Choose herbal tea for calm energy. Move gently — restorative yoga, slow breathing, or a mindful walk in silence. Let your movements reflect peace, not performance.

Today I nourish my body with:

Today I move with intention through:

"I trust the process. I rest in peace. I am aligned with divine flow."

EVENING GRATITUDE

A moment today when I felt deep peace:

DAY 56—AWAKEN & EXPANSION

"I move through life in gratitude and grace."

MORNING RITUAL

Start your morning by placing your hands over your heart. Take three deep breaths — with each inhale, imagine filling yourself with appreciation; with each exhale, release all that feels heavy or unnecessary. Whisper softly:
"Thank you for this breath. Thank you for this moment."
Then, write or speak aloud three things you are grateful for today — big or small.
As you do, feel warmth expanding through your chest.
(This ritual activates your heart's energy field — shifting you into the vibration of abundance, love, and grace.)

_____

JOURNAL REFLECTION

What am I most grateful for in this season of my life?
How does gratitude change the way I experience challenges?
What does grace mean to me — and how can I embody it more fully?
(Today's reflection deepens your connection to grace — the quiet beauty that flows through life when we live in appreciation.)

_____

_____

MEAL & MOVEMENT

Eat mindfully and with appreciation — even a simple meal becomes sacred when received with gratitude. Move with softness — perhaps yoga, a slow walk, or simply stretching while repeating "thank you" for all your body allows you to do.

Today I nourish my body with:

_____

Today I move with intention through:

_____

_____

"My life is filled with blessings. Gratitude opens my heart to grace."

EVENING GRATITUDE

Three moments of grace I experienced today:

_____

_____

DAY 57–AWAKEN & EXPANSION
"I am one with the Divine flow of life."

MORNING RITUAL

Begin your day in quiet reverence. Sit comfortably and close your eyes.
Take three deep, cleansing breaths — inhale peace, exhale surrender.
Visualize a soft light above your head, gently flowing down through your crown,
into your heart, and spreading through your body.
Feel this light connect you to everything — the earth below, the sky above, every
living being around you. Whisper softly: "I am connected to the Divine within
and all around me. I am guided, loved, and supported in every step I take."
Sit in that glow for a few moments, allowing stillness to become presence, and
presence to become peace.
(This ritual deepens spiritual trust — reminding you that connection is your
natural state, not a goal to reach.)

JOURNAL REFLECTION

When do I feel most connected to something greater than myself?
What practices, moments, or environments help me experience that oneness?
How can I bring Divine awareness into ordinary moments of my day?
(Today's reflection reawakens sacred awareness — seeing the divine in yourself,
in others, and in the world around you.)

MEAL & MOVEMENT

Eat reverently — see food as a gift of life energy. Choose simple,
natural meals that make you feel clear and uplifted. Move with
devotion — yoga, mindful walking, or prayerful movement where
each breath becomes communion with the Divine.

Today I nourish my body with:

Today I move with intention through:

> *"I am a vessel of light. I am never alone. I rest in Divine love."*

EVENING GRATITUDE

A moment today when I felt divinely guided or connected:

DAY 58—AWAKEN & EXPANSION

"I honor myself as sacred."

MORNING RITUAL

Begin your morning with a mirror ritual.
Stand before your reflection, take a deep breath, and place a hand over your heart.
Look into your eyes — not critically, but tenderly — and say:
"I love you. You are enough. You are sacred."
Stay present for a few moments, letting any emotion that arises be felt fully — whether it's comfort, resistance, or release.
Then whisper softly:
"I am worthy of the same love I so freely give."
(This ritual reawakens compassion and dissolves separation between who you are and how you treat yourself.)

_____

_____

JOURNAL REFLECTION

When do I feel most connected to something greater than myself?
What practices, moments, or environments help me experience that oneness?
How can I bring Divine awareness into ordinary moments of my day?
(Today's reflection reawakens sacred awareness — seeing the divine in yourself, in others, and in the world around you.)

_____

_____

MEAL & MOVEMENT

Eat with self-respect and presence — nourishing, colorful foods that make you feel alive and cherished. Move with kindness — stretch, dance, or rest depending on what your body needs. Let movement be an act of self-devotion, not discipline.

Today I nourish my body with:

_____

Today I move with intention through:

_____

"I am love. I am light. I am whole."

EVENING GRATITUDE

A moment I practiced self-love today:

_____

_____

DAY 59-AWAKEN & EXPANSION
"I am whole, just as I am."

MORNING RITUAL

Begin by sitting in stillness and taking a deep breath into your belly.
As you exhale, release judgment, tension, and the need to "fix" yourself.
Place one hand on your heart and one on your belly.
Whisper softly:
"Every part of me is welcome here."
"I embrace my light and my shadows with love."
Imagine a soft, golden circle of light forming around you — whole, complete, unbroken.
Breathe into that circle and feel the peace that comes from belonging fully to yourself.
(This ritual awakens radical self-acceptance — the foundation of sustainable peace and authentic expansion.)

JOURNAL REFLECTION

What parts of myself have I struggled to accept or embrace?
What would it look like to love those parts instead of resist them?
How does wholeness feel different from perfection?
(Today's reflection unites self-compassion and awareness — showing that wholeness comes from inclusion, not improvement.)

MEAL & MOVEMENT

Eat meals that balance grounding and vitality — a colorful bowl with grains, greens, and warmth. Move with integration — slow yoga or flowing stretches that connect your breath and body. Let every motion remind you: I am complete.

Today I nourish my body with:

Today I move with intention through:

"I am whole. I am enough.
I am at peace with all that I am."

EVENING GRATITUDE

A part of myself I embraced today:

DAY 60-AWAKEN & EXPANSION
"I flow freely with life."

MORNING RITUAL

Stand tall with your feet grounded and arms relaxed by your sides.

Take three deep breaths, inhaling light and exhaling release.

As you breathe, imagine a river of golden energy flowing through you — effortless, graceful, unstoppable. Whisper softly: "I trust where I am. I move freely with life's rhythm."

Stretch, sway, or dance — even if just for a moment — letting your body move as it wishes. Feel how natural it is to flow when you stop resisting.

(This ritual embodies liberation — the freedom that arises when we surrender control and trust the current of life.)

JOURNAL REFLECTION

What does freedom mean to me now — not as escape, but as presence?
How can I continue to flow with life, even in moments of uncertainty?
What have I discovered about who I am through awakening and expansion?
(Today's reflection seals the energy of this phase — understanding that flow is not what happens to you, it's what happens through you.)

MEAL & MOVEMENT

Eat lightly and intuitively — choose foods that make you feel alive and fluid (like greens, fruit, herbal teas, and nourishing grains). Move in flow — dance, yoga, or even gentle stretching. Let movement mirror ease: fluid, unforced, joyful.

Today I nourish my body with:

Today I move with intention through:

"I am free. I am open. I am in flow with all that is."

EVENING GRATITUDE

A moment today when I felt free or at ease:

DAY 61-MANIFEST & MOMENTUM
"I flow freely with life."

MORNING RITUAL

Begin your day by taking three deep breaths.
As you inhale, feel your body fill with light and possibility.
As you exhale, release distractions or doubts.
Place your hands over your heart and whisper:
"My thoughts, words, and actions are aligned with my purpose."
"What I focus on grows."
Now, write down one clear intention for your day — something meaningful, not rushed.
Visualize that intention already unfolding beautifully, with ease and gratitude.
(This ritual activates manifestation through clarity — a reminder that purpose begins as a seed of focus planted in peace.)

JOURNAL REFLECTION

What am I ready to create or call into my life this month?
Why does this matter to me — what's the deeper purpose beneath the desire?
What small, aligned step can I take today to move toward it?
(Today's reflection brings clarity to creation — shifting focus from wishful thinking to embodied intention.)

MEAL & MOVEMENT

Eat foods that energize creation — whole grains, citrus, greens, and protein-rich meals. Move dynamically — flow yoga, walking meditation, or light strength work. Let your movement feel like momentum building through joy and presence.

Today I nourish my body with:

Today I move with intention through:

"I am the creator of my reality. I manifest through alignment and joy."

EVENING GRATITUDE

One aligned action I took today:

DAY 62-MANIFEST & MOMENTUM

"My energy aligns with my highest vision."

MORNING RITUAL

Find a quiet space and close your eyes.

Take three deep breaths — with each inhale, imagine drawing in golden light; with each exhale, release anything heavy or misaligned.

Now visualize your highest vision — not just what it looks like, but how it feels.

Let yourself feel that emotion fully: peace, joy, freedom, love, abundance. Breathe it into your body as if it already exists.

Whisper softly:

"I vibrate in harmony with what I desire. I am the energy of my vision."

(This ritual teaches that manifestation is not waiting for the future — it's embodying the energy of what you seek, now.)

MEAL & MOVEMENT

Eat high-vibrational meals — fresh produce, water, and foods close to the earth. Move in flow — dance, yoga, or walking while visualizing your dreams. Let movement mirror alignment: effortless, confident, alive.

Today I nourish my body with:

_____

Today I move with intention through:

_____

JOURNAL REFLECTION

How do I want my vision to feel once it's manifested?

Do my thoughts and daily habits reflect that same energy?

What can I shift — emotionally, mentally, or physically — to align more deeply with it today?

(Today's reflection bridges feeling and form — showing that true manifestation begins with energetic coherence.)

_____

_____

"I am in harmony with my purpose. My energy is magnetic to all I desire."

EVENING GRATITUDE

A moment I felt aligned with my vision today:

_____

_____

DAY 63-MANIFEST & MOMENTUM
"My focus is my creative power."

MORNING RITUAL

Begin by sitting in stillness. Take three deep breaths — with each inhale, gather your attention; with each exhale, release distraction.
Visualize your mind as a calm, clear sky, free of clutter.
Now imagine your intention appearing in that sky like sunlight breaking through clouds.
Hold it there with love and clarity for one minute.
Whisper:
"What I focus on grows."
(This ritual sharpens creative awareness — reminding you that clarity is the first step of manifestation.)

_____

JOURNAL REFLECTION

What am I choosing to focus on today?
Do my thoughts reflect what I want to create or what I fear?
How can I gently redirect my attention to faith over doubt?

_____

MEAL & MOVEMENT

Choose meals that enhance focus — whole grains, blueberries, greens, or green tea. Move with direction — yoga or a walk where you repeat your affirmation as a steady rhythm of breath and thought.

Today I nourish my body with:

_____

Today I move with intention through:

_____

"My focus is fertile ground for all I wish to grow."

EVENING GRATITUDE
A thought I chose intentionally today:

_____

DAY 64-MANIFEST & MOMENTUM

"My words create worlds."

MORNING RITUAL

Start your day by speaking three "I am" statements aloud:
I am capable.
I am aligned.
I am becoming everything I dream of.
Pause and feel each statement anchor in your body.
Notice the energy shift — calm, centered, empowered.
Carry those vibrations into your morning conversations.
(This ritual reminds you that language shapes your life — speak from love, not lack.)

JOURNAL REFLECTION

What words do I use often when speaking about my life?
Are they aligned with the reality I want to create?
What new words or mantras will I choose today?

MEAL & MOVEMENT

Choose foods that feel expressive — bright colors and fresh ingredients. Move your energy through sound or voice: hum during your walk or play music that lifts your vibration.

Today I nourish my body with:

Today I move with intention through:

"My words are spells of light. I speak creation into being."

EVENING GRATITUDE

A word or phrase that uplifted me today:

DAY 65-MANIFEST & MOMENTUM
"My belief is magnetic."

MORNING RITUAL

As you wake, take a full breath and say to yourself:
"Everything I believe possible already exists for me."
Close your eyes and visualize a version of yourself who
already lives that belief.
What does their energy feel like? Confident? Grateful?
Peaceful?
Let that feeling take root in your body before you rise.
(This ritual teaches that faith is the bridge between
vision and reality.)

MEAL & MOVEMENT

Eat meals that energize — grains, fruits, and
grounding vegetables. Move in strength — yoga,
stretching, or a mindful workout that connects
effort with faith.

Today I nourish my body with:

Today I move with intention through:

JOURNAL REFLECTION

What belief am I strengthening today?
Where do I still doubt my creative power, and why?
What evidence have I already seen that proves I can
manifest?

"Belief makes all things possible."

EVENING GRATITUDE

A moment I acted from belief today:

DAY 66-MANIFEST & MOMENTUM

"I act with purpose and trust."

MORNING RITUAL

Take a deep breath and ask yourself: "What small step can I take today that aligns with my highest intention?" Wait for a gentle nudge, a spark, or an intuitive idea — it may feel subtle.

Write it down and commit to following through before the day ends.

(This ritual reminds you that inspired action is the meeting point between energy and form.)

JOURNAL REFLECTION

What inspired action am I being guided to take?

How does aligned action feel different from pressure or hustle?

What can I celebrate from today's movement forward?

MEAL & MOVEMENT

Choose meals that fuel momentum — balanced and energizing (like quinoa bowls or smoothies). Move with intention — every motion purposeful, every breath deliberate.

Today I nourish my body with:

Today I move with intention through:

"When I move with purpose, life moves with me."

EVENING GRATITUDE

The inspired action I took today was:

DAY 67-MANIFEST & MOMENTUM

"I trust the unfolding of my desires."

MORNING RITUAL

Take three deep breaths. With each exhale, imagine letting go of control — watching your expectations dissolve like smoke.

Say softly:

"I release the 'how' and trust the 'when. The Universe always delivers what's right for me."

(This ritual frees your energy from resistance, making space for grace.)

_____

_____

JOURNAL REFLECTION

Where am I holding on too tightly to results?

How does surrender create more peace in my process?

What might flow more easily if I stopped forcing it?

_____

_____

MEAL & MOVEMENT

Eat lightly and with calm presence — avoid rushing meals. Move to release tension — long stretches, deep breathing, or gentle flow that mirrors surrender.

Today I nourish my body with:

_____

Today I move with intention through:

_____

"I let go and let flow."

EVENING GRATITUDE

Something I released control over today:

_____

_____

DAY 68-MANIFEST & MOMENTUM

"I am open to miracles, big and small."

MORNING RITUAL

Place both hands over your heart. Take three soft breaths and say aloud: "Today I welcome the unexpected blessings life has prepared for me."
Smile — even slightly — as if the miracle has already happened.
Then move into your morning with openness, ready to notice magic in simple moments.
(This ritual expands your awareness of possibility — miracles are normal when you believe in them.)

MEAL & MOVEMENT

Eat with joy — savor flavors and textures fully. Move playfully — dance, walk, or stretch with gratitude for life's rhythm.

Today I nourish my body with:

_____

Today I move with intention through:

_____

JOURNAL REFLECTION

What miracles (small or large) have I already experienced recently?
How can I become more aware of the magic around me?
What would it feel like to expect miracles daily?

_____

_____

"Every day holds something extraordinary."

EVENING GRATITUDE

A moment that felt like a miracle today:

_____

_____

DAY 69-MANIFEST & MOMENTUM
"Abundance is my natural state."

MORNING RITUAL

Before you rise, place a hand on your heart and say:
"Thank you for all that I have and all that is coming."
Visualize yourself surrounded by light — each beam representing love, opportunities, and resources flowing freely.
Feel gratitude swell in your body.
(This ritual helps you embody abundance now — not later.)

JOURNAL REFLECTION

In what areas of my life do I already feel rich and supported?
Where can I replace scarcity thinking with gratitude?
What does abundance feel like in my body?

MEAL & MOVEMENT

Eat vibrantly — colorful fruits, hearty grains, or a beautifully plated meal. Move expansively — open-arm stretches or a walk outside where you silently thank life with every step.

Today I nourish my body with:

Today I move with intention through:

"Abundance flows through me effortlessly."

EVENING GRATITUDE

One abundant blessing I noticed today:

DAY 70-MANIFEST & MOMENTUM

"I honor the rhythm of my energy and creativity."

MORNING RITUAL

Upon waking, sit up slowly and take a deep, grounding breath.
Ask yourself gently: "What is my energy asking for today — action or rest?"
Place a hand over your heart and whisper: "I honor where I am."
Whether your answer is movement, stillness, or reflection, commit to respecting it fully today.
(This ritual reminds you that rest and creation exist in the same sacred cycle — both are vital for manifestation.)

JOURNAL REFLECTION

What is my current energy level and how can I work with it, not against it?

How do I feel when I rest vs. when I push?

How can I give myself permission to flow with my natural rhythm?

MEAL & MOVEMENT

Eat intuitively based on your energy — warming soups if tired, fresh greens if active. Move in harmony with your body's rhythm — slow stretching or powerful flow, depending on your vitality.

Today I nourish my body with:

Today I move with intention through:

"I flow with my natural cycles. Balance is creation in motion."

EVENING GRATITUDE

One way I honored my energy today:

TRUEJOY-LIVING

A YEAR OF TRANSFORMATION

DAY 71–MANIFEST & MOMENTUM

"I feel my dreams as if they are already real."

MORNING RITUAL

Close your eyes and take three deep breaths. Visualize your dream life vividly — not as an observer, but as if you're living it right now.

See the colors, sounds, and details. Feel the emotions — joy, peace, gratitude.

Whisper softly: "My feelings fuel my creations."

Stay in that vibration for one minute.

(This ritual turns imagination into energy — emotion is the magnet that attracts form.)

JOURNAL REFLECTION

What emotions do I want to feel when my vision is realized?

How can I bring those same feelings into today?

What parts of my dream already exist in my current life?

MEAL & MOVEMENT

Eat foods that inspire pleasure and vibrancy — colorful fruits, aromatic teas, or spices that awaken the senses. Move with fluidity — dance or yoga that expresses emotion.

Today I nourish my body with:

_____

Today I move with intention through:

_____

"I feel it. I believe it. I am it."

EVENING GRATITUDE

A moment today that matched my desired feelings:

_____

_____

DAY 72-MANIFEST & MOMENTUM

"My intuition leads me to alignment."

MORNING RITUAL

Sit quietly and breathe into your heart space.
Ask inwardly: "What does my intuition want me to know today?"
Don't think — feel. Notice sensations, ideas, or emotions that arise.
Whisper: "I trust my inner guidance."
Follow one small intuitive nudge today, even if it feels simple — like calling someone, taking a walk, or saying no.
(This ritual teaches trust in subtle inner whispers — intuition is the compass of manifestation.)

JOURNAL REFLECTION

What intuitive message came to me today?
How did I honor it?
How can I tell the difference between fear and intuition?

MEAL & MOVEMENT

Eat what your body requests intuitively — not by habit.
Move in silence to listen inwardly: walk, stretch, or flow without music.

Today I nourish my body with:

Today I move with intention through:

"My inner voice always leads me home."

EVENING GRATITUDE

A moment I followed my intuition:

TRUEJOY-LIVING

A YEAR OF TRANSFORMATION

DAY 73-MANIFEST & MOMENTUM

"My space supports my success."

MORNING RITUAL

Before beginning your day, look around your space.
Ask: "Does this environment reflect my dreams?"
Take five minutes to clear, rearrange, or beautify one small area.
Light a candle, open a window, or add a flower.
Whisper: "My outer world reflects my inner peace."
(This ritual grounds your manifestation energy in physical reality — your space becomes a mirror of your vision.)

MEAL & MOVEMENT

Eat in a clean, calm setting — create beauty around your meal. Move through your space with intention — tidy, stretch, or dance while breathing gratitude into your home.

Today I nourish my body with:

Today I move with intention through:

JOURNAL REFLECTION

How does my environment affect my energy?
What can I add, remove, or rearrange to reflect who I'm becoming?
How does order or beauty support my manifestation process?

"My space is sacred. My home supports my dreams."

EVENING GRATITUDE

A shift I made in my space today:

TRUEJOY-LIVING
A YEAR OF TRANSFORMATION

DAY 74 - MANIFEST & MOMENTUM
"Joy is my magnet."

MORNING RITUAL

Smile — even before you rise. Take a deep breath and say aloud:
"I choose joy as my frequency today."
Think of one small thing that makes you happy — music, a walk, a favorite drink — and schedule it intentionally.
Make joy a priority, not an afterthought.
(This ritual teaches that joy is productive energy — it amplifies all creation.)

JOURNAL REFLECTION

What brings me genuine joy right now?
How can I infuse my day with that feeling?
How does joy change my energy and perspective?

MEAL & MOVEMENT

Eat what delights you — nourish body and spirit.
Move playfully — dance, skip, or flow freely without rules.

Today I nourish my body with:

_____

Today I move with intention through:

_____

"Joy leads me to everything meant for me."

EVENING GRATITUDE

A joyful moment I experienced today:

_____

_____

DAY 75-MANIFEST & MOMENTUM

"I thank life for blessings on their way."

MORNING RITUAL

Write down three desires you're calling in.
Next to each, write "Thank you for this already being mine."
Close your eyes, take a deep breath, and feel gratitude as if it's already happened.
(This ritual shifts you into alignment with receiving — gratitude bridges desire and manifestation.)

MEAL & MOVEMENT

Eat with appreciation for nourishment and effort behind your meal. Move with thankfulness — walk or stretch while mentally saying "thank you" for your body's strength.

Today I nourish my body with:

Today I move with intention through:

JOURNAL REFLECTION

What am I most thankful for that hasn't yet arrived?
How does gratitude change my level of trust?
How can I thank life more freely, even in uncertainty?

"Thank you, Universe, for blessings both seen and unseen."

EVENING GRATITUDE

A moment I felt deep appreciation today:

TRUEJOY-LIVING

A YEAR OF TRANSFORMATION

DAY 76–MANIFEST & MOMENTUM

"I live as my highest self now."

MORNING RITUAL

Close your eyes and picture your future self — radiant, peaceful, successful, fulfilled. Ask: "How would she move, speak, choose, and care for herself today?"

Then embody that version in one small way — your posture, tone, routine, or boundary.

Let your actions align with who you're becoming.

(This ritual makes manifestation tangible — by being the energy, you become the reality.)

JOURNAL REFLECTION

Who is my highest self?

What habits, language, or mindset can I adopt to live as her now?

How does embodying her energy change the way I feel today?

MEAL & MOVEMENT

Eat as your highest self would — nourishing and balanced. Move with confidence — posture tall, breath steady, presence strong.

Today I nourish my body with:

_____

Today I move with intention through:

_____

"I am becoming who I am meant to be — one aligned choice at a time."

EVENING GRATITUDE

One way I embodied my higher self today:

_____

_____

TRUEJOY-LIVING

A YEAR OF TRANSFORMATION

DAY 77-MANIFEST & MOMENTUM

"Old stories no longer define me."

MORNING RITUAL

Take a slow, deep breath in, then exhale completely.
Place your hand on your heart and whisper:
"I am safe to see what no longer serves me."
Visualize old thoughts or fears floating up like bubbles — beliefs
such as "It's too late," "I'm not ready," "I'm not enough."
As each bubble rises, imagine it popping and releasing light
instead of limitation.
(This ritual clears energetic space for new truth to take root.)

MEAL & MOVEMENT

Eat cleansing, fresh meals — greens, citrus, or herbal teas
to release stagnant energy. Move to let go — shaking,
stretching, or a slow flow focused on exhaling tension.

Today I nourish my body with:

Today I move with intention through:

JOURNAL REFLECTION

What beliefs or patterns keep me small or stuck?

Where did they come from — and do they still serve me?

What new empowering truth am I choosing to believe
instead?

*"I am free to think new thoughts.
I am limitless."*

EVENING GRATITUDE

A limiting belief I released today:

DAY 78-MANIFEST & MOMENTUM

"I trust that everything is unfolding perfectly."

MORNING RITUAL

Before you move from bed, place your hand over your heart.

Whisper: "Even what I can't see is working for me."
Take three calm breaths, visualizing yourself walking a bright path ahead — you can't see every step, but you feel deeply supported with each one. (This ritual builds patience and faith — the soil where manifestations root and grow.)

JOURNAL REFLECTION

Where am I being invited to trust more deeply?
What evidence do I already have that life supports me?
How can I stay grounded in patience today?

MEAL & MOVEMENT

Eat grounding foods — rice, oats, root vegetables — to stabilize trust. Move with mindfulness — a slow walk or breath-led stretching to feel guided by rhythm, not rush.

Today I nourish my body with:

Today I move with intention through:

"I am guided, protected, and exactly where I'm meant to be."

EVENING GRATITUDE

A moment today that reminded me to trust:

TRUEJOY-LIVING

A YEAR OF TRANSFORMATION

DAY 79-MANIFEST & MOMENTUM
"Confidence is my natural state."

MORNING RITUAL
Stand in front of a mirror.
Look yourself in the eyes and smile.
Take one strong, deep breath and say aloud:
"I am powerful. I am enough. I am radiant."
Roll your shoulders back, lift your chin slightly, and
hold your stance — feel your strength without tension.
(This ritual anchors confidence as energy, not ego —
quiet, steady, and sure.)

JOURNAL REFLECTION
What does confidence feel like in my body?
When have I felt most powerful and at ease?
What daily action helps me stay in that vibration?

MEAL & MOVEMENT
Eat meals that strengthen and energize — protein,
colorful vegetables, and water. Move powerfully — yoga
flows, walking tall, or standing meditations that embody
grounded confidence.

Today I nourish my body with:

Today I move with intention through:

*"I shine with quiet confidence.
My light uplifts others."*

EVENING GRATITUDE
Embodying confidence helped me feel:

DAY 80-MANIFEST & MOMENTUM

"I am open to abundance in all forms."

MORNING RITUAL

Sit with your palms open on your lap. Take three deep breaths, saying silently: "I am open. I am worthy. I receive with ease."

Visualize golden light pouring into your open hands — gifts from the Universe flowing toward you with love.

Let gratitude fill your heart as you whisper: "I allow blessings to find me easily."

(This ritual balances giving with receiving — a vital key in manifesting abundance.)

JOURNAL REFLECTION

In what areas of my life do I resist receiving support or abundance?

What would it look like to open my heart to more?

How can I practice receiving today?

MEAL & MOVEMENT

Eat slowly, savoring every bite — receive nourishment fully. Move gently and receptively — yin yoga, stretching, or rest. Allow your body to feel supported, not rushed.

Today I nourish my body with:

Today I move with intention through:

"I receive with grace, gratitude, and joy."

EVENING GRATITUDE

A gift, compliment, or opportunity I received today:

TRUEJOY-LIVING

A YEAR OF TRANSFORMATION

DAY 81-MANIFEST & MOMENTUM

"Every step forward is success."

MORNING RITUAL

Before starting your day, reflect on three recent moments of progress — no matter how small. Smile and whisper:

"I am proud of myself."

Close your eyes and feel that pride expand through your chest like warmth.

(This ritual builds momentum by acknowledging growth — gratitude turns progress into power.)

JOURNAL REFLECTION

What am I proud of today?

How can I celebrate myself more often?

How does appreciation fuel my motivation?

MEAL & MOVEMENT

Eat something that feels like celebration — vibrant and joyful. Move with playfulness — dance, stretch, or take a light walk with music you love.

Today I nourish my body with:

Today I move with intention through:

"I celebrate progress. I honor my becoming."

EVENING GRATITUDE

A win I celebrated today:

TRUEJOY-LIVING

A YEAR OF TRANSFORMATION

DAY 82-MANIFEST & MOMENTUM

"I trust the timing of my dreams."

MORNING RITUAL

Take three soft breaths. As you inhale, feel patience fill your body; as you exhale, release urgency. Whisper: "Everything blooms in its perfect season." Visualize your dreams as seeds already planted, growing unseen but steadily beneath the surface. (This ritual restores trust in divine timing — easing the need for control.)

JOURNAL REFLECTION

Where in my life am I rushing the process?
What has unfolded beautifully once I stopped forcing it?
How can I create space for patience and trust today?

MEAL & MOVEMENT

Eat slowly, mindfully, and without multitasking. Move with grace — tai chi, slow yoga, or walking at your natural pace to honor life's rhythm.

Today I nourish my body with:

Today I move with intention through:

"My dreams are growing right on time."

EVENING GRATITUDE

Something that unfolded perfectly today:

TRUEJOY-LIVING

A YEAR OF TRANSFORMATION

DAY 83-MANIFEST & MOMENTUM
"My prosperity supports my purpose."

MORNING RITUAL

Place both hands on your heart. Take three deep breaths and say softly: "Money is energy. I use it with love and intention."

Visualize your income and resources circulating like golden light — moving through your life with purpose and flow.

(This ritual connects abundance to alignment — money as a mirror of meaning.)

JOURNAL REFLECTION

How does money currently reflect my values and energy?

What beliefs about money am I ready to rewrite?

How can I use my resources to serve both joy and purpose?

MEAL & MOVEMENT

Eat mindfully and with gratitude for provision. Move with grounded awareness — slow steps, steady breath, embodying stability and flow.

Today I nourish my body with:

Today I move with intention through:

"My abundance serves love, growth, and good."

EVENING GRATITUDE

One way I used my resources meaningfully today:

TRUEJOY-LIVING

A YEAR OF TRANSFORMATION

DAY 84-MANIFEST & MOMENTUM

"When I give from love. I receive in flow."

MORNING RITUAL

Place your hands together at your heart in a gesture of
gratitude. Take three deep breaths and whisper:
"May everything I do today be of benefit to others."
Visualize your energy radiating outward — each action,
word, or smile sending ripples of light through the
world.
(This ritual reminds you that generosity expands your
energetic flow — giving and receiving are one continuous
breath.)

MEAL & MOVEMENT

Eat meals you can share — invite connection through
food. Move with others or in service — help, support, or
simply walk mindfully while wishing blessings to everyone
you pass.

Today I nourish my body with:

Today I move with intention through:

JOURNAL REFLECTION

How can I serve today without depleting myself?
What does "giving from overflow" mean to me?
How has service already brought abundance into my life?

*"My service is sacred. My heart
and the Universe work as one."*

EVENING GRATITUDE

One way I served with love today:

DAY 85—MANIFEST & MOMENTUM

"Consistency turns dreams into reality."

MORNING RITUAL

Revisit your journal or intentions from the start of this phase.

Read them slowly, out loud, and feel how much closer they already are.

Whisper: "Each small step compounds into transformation."

(This ritual re-anchors commitment — showing that success is built through steady presence, not bursts of effort.)

MEAL & MOVEMENT

Eat nourishing, balanced meals that sustain energy — think steady fuel over stimulation. Move rhythmically — a jog, yoga, or flow that builds endurance and focus.

Today I nourish my body with:

Today I move with intention through:

JOURNAL REFLECTION

Which daily practices have supported my momentum the most?

Where can I strengthen my consistency with ease, not pressure?

What reminder keeps me devoted to my vision?

"My commitment creates my reality."

EVENING GRATITUDE

A consistent habit I honored today:

DAY 86–MANIFEST & MOMENTUM

"Gratitude is the heartbeat of manifestation."

MORNING RITUAL

Begin your day by looking around and naming three things you once desired that are now part of your life.

Place your hands over your heart and whisper: "Thank you for what has already blossomed."

(This ritual transforms appreciation into expansion — what you bless, grows.)

JOURNAL REFLECTION

What manifestations have already come true for me?

How can I nurture them with attention and gratitude?

How does appreciation deepen my sense of abundance?

MEAL & MOVEMENT

Eat mindfully, savoring every bite. Move with gratitude — during stretches or walks, mentally thank your body for all it allows you to experience.

Today I nourish my body with:

Today I move with intention through:

"Thank you for all that is and all that's coming."

EVENING GRATITUDE

One manifestation I celebrated today:

DAY 87–MANIFEST & MOMENTUM

"There is always more than enough."

MORNING RITUAL

Take a deep breath and visualize your life as an ocean — vast, full, and infinite.
Whisper softly:
"I live in a limitless Universe."
Smile and notice how this truth relaxes your mind and opens your heart.
(This ritual retrains the subconscious for overflow — turning fear of lack into trust in plenty.)

JOURNAL REFLECTION

What are my first thoughts when I think about abundance or wealth?
How can I affirm "there is enough" in daily choices?
Where can I act as if my supply is infinite today?

MEAL & MOVEMENT

Eat without guilt or rush — abundance is in permission, not excess. Move expansively — stretch, reach, or flow with open arms to welcome abundance.

Today I nourish my body with:

Today I move with intention through:

"I am abundance in motion."

EVENING GRATITUDE

A moment today that reflected abundance:

TRUEJOY-LIVING

A YEAR OF TRANSFORMATION

DAY 88-MANIFEST & MOMENTUM

"I am rooted in peace as I expand."

MORNING RITUAL

Stand with bare feet on the ground or floor.
Breathe deeply and imagine roots growing from
your feet into the earth.
Whisper: "I stay steady as I grow."
Visualize golden light traveling from earth to
crown — connecting stability and expansion.
(This ritual ensures balance — reminding you that
growth is strongest when rooted.)

JOURNAL REFLECTION

How do I stay centered while expanding?
What daily practices keep me balanced amidst
momentum?
How does grounding support my creativity?

MEAL & MOVEMENT

Eat earthy foods — grains, root vegetables, lentils. Move
deliberately — slow grounding yoga or deep squats to
reconnect to your center.

Today I nourish my body with:

Today I move with intention through:

"I am both the root and the bloom."

EVENING GRATITUDE

A moment I felt grounded today:

DAY 89-MANIFEST & MOMENTUM

"The Universe and I create together in harmony."

MORNING RITUAL

Place a hand over your heart and another toward the sky.
Take three deep breaths and whisper: "I am in partnership with life itself."
Visualize your intentions floating upward like lanterns, received and guided by the Universe.
(This ritual reawakens co-creation — trust in divine collaboration rather than solitary effort.)

MEAL & MOVEMENT

Eat intuitively — let your body guide portions and pace. Move fluidly — yoga or flowing dance symbolizing give and receive.

Today I nourish my body with:

_____

Today I move with intention through:

_____

JOURNAL REFLECTION

How does it feel to see the Universe as my creative partner?
What signs or synchronicities have affirmed my path recently?
How can I stay open to guidance today?

_____

_____

"I trust the divine choreography of my life."

EVENING GRATITUDE

A sign or message I noticed today:

_____

_____

DAY 90-MANIFEST & MOMENTUM

"Creation flows easily through me."

MORNING RITUAL

Take three luxurious breaths, smiling softly with
each inhale.
Say aloud:
"I am in harmony with the rhythm of creation."
Move gently — stretch, sway, or dance for one
minute with eyes closed, feeling joy ripple through
every cell.
(This ritual celebrates integration — you are no
longer "doing" manifestation; you are living it.)

JOURNAL REFLECTION

What have I learned about the art of manifestation?
How does ease feel compared to striving?
What does "flow" mean to me now?

MEAL & MOVEMENT

Eat something that feels like celebration — beautiful,
nourishing, and joyful. Move freely — dance, flow, or walk
in gratitude for how far you've come.

Today I nourish my body with:

Today I move with intention through:

*"I am in harmony with life. I create
through joy."*

EVENING GRATITUDE

A moment of flow or ease I experienced today:

DAY 91-Release & Renewal

"I release with gratitude and love."

MORNING RITUAL

Find a quiet space. Take three deep breaths and whisper:
"I am safe to let go." Visualize old patterns, worries, or
stories as leaves falling gently from a tree — each one
representing something you're ready to release. As they
touch the ground, feel lightness returning to your body.
(This ritual begins the evolution process — releasing
what no longer fits the person you are becoming.)

MEAL & MOVEMENT

Choose cleansing meals — soups, greens, lemon
water. Move to release — gentle twisting yoga or a
brisk walk to reset your energy.

Today I nourish my body with:

Today I move with intention through:

JOURNAL REFLECTION

What habits, relationships, or beliefs am I ready to
release?
How can I honor what these experiences taught me
before letting them go?
How does release create room for renewal?

"In releasing, I make space for my evolution."

EVENING GRATITUDE

Something I released today:

DAY 92-Release & Renewal
"Forgiveness frees me."

MORNING RITUAL

Take a slow, deep breath in, feeling your heart expand.
As you exhale, silently say: "I choose peace over resentment."
If someone or something comes to mind, visualize sending them (or yourself) light — not to excuse, but to release the hold it has on you.
(This ritual dissolves energetic cords of tension — forgiveness is freedom, not approval.)

JOURNAL REFLECTION

Who or what am I ready to forgive?
How has holding on kept me tied to pain?
What would freedom through forgiveness feel like?

MEAL & MOVEMENT

Eat comforting, heart-opening meals — soups, tea, or cacao. Move gently — slow heart-opening yoga or deep-breath stretches.

Today I nourish my body with:

_____

Today I move with intention through:

_____

"I forgive. I free. I evolve."

EVENING GRATITUDE

A person or situation I released through forgiveness:

_____

_____

DAY 93-Release & Renewal
"Every feeling has wisdom to offer."

MORNING RITUAL
Sit quietly and place one hand on your heart, the other on your belly. Ask:
"What emotion lives in me today?"
Whatever arises — joy, sadness, anger, calm — greet it without judgment.
Whisper: "Thank you for your message."
(This ritual helps participants move from resisting emotions to receiving their lessons.)

JOURNAL REFLECTION
What emotion am I feeling most strongly today?
What might this feeling be trying to teach or show me?
How can I allow it to move through me with compassion?

MEAL & MOVEMENT
Eat intuitively based on your emotional state — grounding foods if overwhelmed, lighter meals if heavy. Move with emotion — flow, walk, or even dance through what you feel.

Today I nourish my body with:

Today I move with intention through:

"I am safe to feel. I am open to learn."

EVENING GRATITUDE
An emotion I honored today:

DAY 94–Release & Renewal

"I grow beyond my comfort zone with courage."

MORNING RITUAL

As you begin your day, stand tall, take a deep breath, and say aloud: "I am ready to grow."
Visualize yourself stepping through a doorway of light — symbolizing courage and expansion.
Smile, even if you feel uncertain.
(This ritual builds resilience — growth and ease rarely coexist, yet evolution is worth the stretch.)

JOURNAL REFLECTION

What area of my life is calling me to stretch?
What fears arise when I step outside comfort?
How will I support myself through that growth?

MEAL & MOVEMENT

Eat energizing meals — whole grains, seeds, bright fruits. Move boldly — something slightly challenging like a new workout, dance, or longer walk.

Today I nourish my body with:

Today I move with intention through:

"Growth is my nature, and I trust the process."

EVENING GRATITUDE

A growth moment I embraced today:

DAY 95-Release & Renewal

"I release control and trust the flow of life."

MORNING RITUAL

Take three deep breaths. With each inhale, say: "I receive."
With each exhale, say: "I release."
Imagine holding a handful of sand — the tighter you grip, the more escapes. Now loosen your hand, allowing the grains to settle naturally.
(This ritual teaches peaceful detachment — life flows best when not forced.)

JOURNAL REFLECTION

Where am I clinging too tightly to control?
What could unfold if I trusted more deeply?
What does surrender look like in daily life?

MEAL & MOVEMENT

Eat lightly and simply — avoid over-planning. Move with surrender — yin yoga, stretching, or slow breathing.

Today I nourish my body with:

Today I move with intention through:

"I trust the rhythm of my evolution."

EVENING GRATITUDE

A situation I let flow naturally today:

DAY 96–Release & Renewal

"Change is the path to transformation."

MORNING RITUAL

Light a candle or take three deep breaths.
Whisper: "I welcome change as a friend."
Visualize yourself shedding an old layer — stepping
out of what's outdated and into the new energy
waiting for you.
Feel renewal rush in like fresh air.
(This ritual reframes change as sacred evolution,
not chaos.)

MEAL & MOVEMENT

Eat something new — try a flavor or recipe you've never
had. Move in a different way — explore variety to
symbolize adaptability.

Today I nourish my body with:

_____

Today I move with intention through:

_____

JOURNAL REFLECTION

What changes are happening in my life right now?
How can I meet them with openness instead of
resistance?
What is this change preparing me for?

_____

_____

"Change renews me. I flow with transformation."

EVENING GRATITUDE

A change I accepted today:

_____

_____

TRUEJOY-LIVING

A YEAR OF TRANSFORMATION

DAY 97–Release & Renewal

"Peace is my natural state."

MORNING RITUAL

Before you check your phone or start your tasks,
take three slow breaths and smile gently.
Whisper: "I choose peace over urgency."
Sit in stillness for one minute, simply breathing
and noticing.
Let peace rise naturally from within.
(This ritual reminds you that peace is not found —
it's remembered.)

MEAL & MOVEMENT

Eat calming foods — herbal teas, soups,
gentle flavors. Move slowly — restorative
yoga, meditation, or a nature walk.

Today I nourish my body with:

_____

Today I move with intention through:

_____

JOURNAL REFLECTION

What disturbs my peace most often, and how can I
respond differently?
What practices instantly bring me back to calm?
How can I prioritize serenity today?

_____

_____

*"Change renews me. I flow
with transformation."*

EVENING GRATITUDE

A peaceful moment I experienced today:

_____

_____

DAY 98–Emotional Mastery & Renewal

"I witness my life with compassion and clarity."

MORNING RITUAL

Take three deep breaths. As you exhale, imagine
creating space between you and your thoughts.
Say softly: "I am the observer, not the storm."
Visualize watching clouds drift across the sky —
each one a passing thought or feeling. You do not
chase or change them; you simply witness.
(This ritual cultivates emotional awareness without
attachment — the foundation of self-mastery.)

JOURNAL REFLECTION

What emotions or thoughts have I observed today?
How does it feel to witness them without
judgment?
What truths emerge when I stop labeling
experiences as "good" or "bad"?

MEAL & MOVEMENT

Eat slowly and mindfully — noticing colors, textures,
and sensations. Move meditatively — walking or
stretching in silence, observing your breath as an
anchor.

Today I nourish my body with:

Today I move with intention through:

Awareness is peace. I rest in understanding.

EVENING GRATITUDE

Something I observed calmly today:

TRUEJOY-LIVING

A YEAR OF TRANSFORMATION

DAY 99-Emotional Mastery & Renewal
"I am enough in every phase of becoming."

MORNING RITUAL

Stand before a mirror.
Place a hand over your heart and whisper:
"I accept myself completely — here, now, in this moment."
Take three slow breaths and allow relief to flow through you.
You are not behind; you are unfolding perfectly.
(This ritual rebuilds self-worth through unconditional acceptance.)

JOURNAL REFLECTION

What part of myself needs more acceptance and kindness?
How do I speak to myself when I'm struggling?
What would I say to a friend feeling the same way?

MEAL & MOVEMENT

Eat foods that comfort and nourish — oatmeal, soup, warm tea. Move softly — gentle yoga, a mindful walk, or a stretch that says "thank you" to your body.

Today I nourish my body with:

Today I move with intention through:

"I am whole. I am worthy. I am enough."

EVENING GRATITUDE

One thing I accepted about myself today:

TRUEJOY-LIVING
A YEAR OF TRANSFORMATION

DAY 100-Emotional Mastery & Renewal

"My emotions flow in harmony with peace."

MORNING RITUAL

Sit comfortably and close your eyes.
Take a deep breath, imagining a scale within your chest
balancing — one side emotion, the other wisdom.
Whisper: "I feel deeply, yet stay centered."
(This ritual helps you integrate feeling and awareness — the art
of balance.)

JOURNAL REFLECTION

What emotion feels strongest today?
How can I honor it without being swept away?
What helps me stay centered in emotional waves?

MEAL & MOVEMENT

Eat stabilizing meals — complex carbs, water, balanced portions.
Move rhythmically — steady yoga, swimming, or any flow that
connects emotion and breath.

Today I nourish my body with:

_____

Today I move with intention through:

_____

"I flow with life's tides, anchored in peace."

EVENING GRATITUDE

An emotion I balanced with grace today:

_____

_____

DAY 101–Emotional Mastery & Renewal
"I bend but do not break."

MORNING RITUAL

Place both feet on the ground and take three grounding breaths.
Say softly: "I am strong enough for this moment."
Visualize your energy as a tree — roots deep, branches flexible.
Feel strength and softness coexist within you.
(This ritual connects stability with adaptability — resilience through presence.)

MEAL & MOVEMENT

Eat energizing, earthy foods — sweet potatoes, greens, grains. Move with strength — walking with intention or light resistance work.

Today I nourish my body with:

Today I move with intention through:

JOURNAL REFLECTION

How have I proven my resilience in the past?
What helps me stay strong in challenge?
How can I nurture recovery as much as effort?

"I am unshakable in my truth."

EVENING GRATITUDE

A moment of strength I noticed today:

DAY 102-Emotional Mastery & Renewal

"My presence matters more than performance."

MORNING RITUAL

As you begin your day, take one slow breath and whisper:
"I release the need to prove."
Move intentionally through your morning — feel water on your hands, smell your coffee or tea, notice sunlight.
Remind yourself: This is enough.
(This ritual softens the pressure of perfectionism, grounding you in being over doing.)

_____

JOURNAL REFLECTION

Where in my life do I chase perfection?
How can I bring more presence to those areas instead?
What does "enough" look like for me today?

_____

_____

MEAL & MOVEMENT

Eat without multitasking — one mindful meal in silence. Move simply — stretch, walk, or breathe deeply without chasing results.

Today I nourish my body with:

_____

Today I move with intention through:

_____

"Presence is perfection."

EVENING GRATITUDE

A moment of presence I experienced today:

_____

_____

DAY 103-Emotional Mastery & Renewal

"I choose calm over chaos."

MORNING RITUAL

Before you begin your day, take three slow breaths.

Imagine a small pause between stimulus and response — a soft golden light of awareness.

Whisper: "I respond from love, not reaction."

(This ritual strengthens emotional regulation — cultivating peace in moments of tension.)

JOURNAL REFLECTION

What triggers reactive emotions in me?

How can I build more space between feeling and reacting?

What would responding with love look like today?

MEAL & MOVEMENT

Eat balanced, steady meals — avoid caffeine if tense. Move in flow — walks or yoga to keep energy calm and grounded.

Today I nourish my body with:

Today I move with intention through:

"Love is my first language."

EVENING GRATITUDE

A moment I chose love over reaction:

DAY 104-Emotional Mastery & Renewal

"Healing unfolds in perfect time."

MORNING RITUAL

Place a hand over your heart and whisper:
"I give myself permission to heal."
Take a deep breath and visualize light slowly filling every part of your body — healing, soothing, restoring balance.
There's no rush; healing is a rhythm, not a race.
(This ritual shifts you from forcing healing to allowing it — gentle acceptance over urgency.)

JOURNAL REFLECTION

What part of me still needs compassion and care?
How can I nurture healing without impatience?
What signs of progress can I already see within me?

MEAL & MOVEMENT

Eat restorative meals — soups, herbal teas, gentle foods. Move softly — restorative yoga, stretching, or a slow nature walk.

Today I nourish my body with:

Today I move with intention through:

"I am healing, whole, and held in love."

EVENING GRATITUDE

A healing moment I noticed today:

TRUEJOY-LIVING

A YEAR OF TRANSFORMATION

DAY 105-Renewal, Purpose & Empowerment

"My purpose is a living expression of my truth."

MORNING RITUAL

Sit quietly and place both hands over your heart.
Take three slow breaths, then ask yourself: "What lights me up from within?"
Listen for a whisper — a feeling, image, or memory — not a logical answer.
Your purpose speaks softly through joy, not pressure.
(This ritual rekindles connection to inner direction, reminding you that purpose unfolds naturally as you live authentically.)

JOURNAL REFLECTION

What moments make me feel most aligned and alive?
What does "purpose" feel like — not just sound like — in my body?
How can I express my purpose through small daily actions?

MEAL & MOVEMENT

Eat energizing, joyful foods — bright colors, fresh flavors.
Move with intention — dance, yoga, or walking while reflecting on what makes you feel alive.

Today I nourish my body with:

Today I move with intention through:

"I am guided by joy, not obligation."

EVENING GRATITUDE

One way I lived with purpose today:

DAY 106-Renewal, Purpose & Empowerment

"The answers I seek are already within me."

MORNING RITUAL

Take three slow breaths. As you exhale, place a hand over your heart and whisper: "I trust my inner knowing." Close your eyes and imagine a golden light at the center of your chest — your intuition glowing quietly, steady and sure.
Ask it one simple question about today, and wait for the first feeling or thought that arises.
(This ritual reawakens self-trust — intuition is the voice of your evolved self.)

JOURNAL REFLECTION

What intuitive nudges have I ignored in the past and why?
How can I listen and act more confidently today?
What evidence shows that my inner wisdom is trustworthy?

MEAL & MOVEMENT

Eat intuitively — choose what feels nourishing, not what you "should" eat. Move with inner guidance — walk, stretch, or dance following your body's lead.

Today I nourish my body with:

Today I move with intention through:

"My inner wisdom always leads me home."

EVENING GRATITUDE

A moment I trusted my intuition today:

DAY 107-Renewal, Purpose & Empowerment
"My truth is safe to be seen."

MORNING RITUAL

Before speaking or posting today, pause and ask:
"Is this my truth?"
Take a breath and feel your throat soften. Say
aloud: "It's safe to be real."
Throughout the day, express from honesty and love
— whether through words, art, or action.
(This ritual reclaims self-expression as sacred —
authenticity fuels evolution.)

JOURNAL REFLECTION

Where do I still hide or edit my truth?
What would full authenticity look and feel like for
me?
How does expressing truth strengthen my
confidence?

MEAL & MOVEMENT

Eat freely — savor each bite without self-judgment. Move
expressively — dance, stretch, or sing to open your voice
and body.

Today I nourish my body with:

_____

Today I move with intention through:

_____

"Authenticity is freedom"

EVENING GRATITUDE

One moment I spoke or acted authentically today:

_____

_____

DAY 108-Renewal, Purpose & Empowerment

"I give myself grace as I grow."

MORNING RITUAL

Sit comfortably and place both hands over your heart.
Take a deep breath and whisper:
"I'm doing my best — and that is enough."
Visualize wrapping yourself in soft golden light —
comfort, forgiveness, and warmth surrounding every
part of you.
(This ritual reinforces that compassion is the gentle
strength of evolution — you grow best when you feel safe
inside yourself.)

JOURNAL REFLECTION

How do I speak to myself when I make mistakes?
What would compassion look like in my daily self-talk?
How can I give myself more grace today?

MEAL & MOVEMENT

Eat soothing meals — warm, nourishing, simple. Move
softly — restorative yoga, stretching, or a slow walk in
nature.

Today I nourish my body with:

Today I move with intention through:

"Grace is my growth partner."

EVENING GRATITUDE

A moment I chose kindness over criticism:

TRUEJOY-LIVING

A YEAR OF TRANSFORMATION

DAY 109-Renewal, Purpose & Empowerment
"Boundaries protect my peace and power."

MORNING RITUAL

Take a deep breath and visualize a soft, glowing light surrounding your body — not a wall, but a loving boundary.

Whisper: "I choose where my energy flows."

Throughout the day, notice what drains or uplifts your energy — adjust with love.

(This ritual redefines boundaries as compassion in motion — for self and others.)

JOURNAL REFLECTION

Where do I need clearer boundaries?

How can I communicate them with love, not defense?

How do boundaries create more freedom for connection?

MEAL & MOVEMENT

Eat grounding meals — root vegetables, lentils, teas. Move in a way that reinforces sovereignty — standing poses or mindful walking.

Today I nourish my body with:

_____

Today I move with intention through:

_____

"My boundaries are sacred acts of self-love."

EVENING GRATITUDE

Protecting my peace helped me feel:

_____

_____

DAY 110-Renewal, Purpose & Empowerment
"I create my life through conscious choice."

MORNING RITUAL

Stand tall, take three breaths, and whisper: "I am the author of my story."
Visualize yourself at a crossroads — one path leads to fear, the other to empowerment. Choose empowerment consciously and step forward in your mind's eye.
(This ritual awakens free will and responsibility — evolution thrives on awareness in action.)

_____

JOURNAL REFLECTION

What decision today can I make from empowerment, not habit?
How do I reclaim authorship over my choices?
What does it mean to choose with awareness?

_____

_____

MEAL & MOVEMENT

Eat energizing meals that fuel clear thinking — greens, citrus, whole grains. Move powerfully — walking with intention, confident posture, steady breath.

Today I nourish my body with:

_____

Today I move with intention through:

_____

"Each choice I make shapes my destiny."

EVENING GRATITUDE

A conscious choice I made today:

_____

_____

DAY 111-Renewal, Purpose & Empowerment

"Every step I've taken has led me here."

MORNING RITUAL

Look back gently at your journey so far. Place a hand over your heart and whisper: "I honor how far I've come."
Smile as you recall the lessons, the resilience, and the love you've cultivated.
You are the living proof of transformation.
(This ritual grounds you in gratitude and acknowledgment — celebration anchors evolution.)

JOURNAL REFLECTION

What changes in myself am I most proud of?
How does celebrating progress deepen my motivation?
What does it mean to evolve with joy?

MEAL & MOVEMENT

Eat celebratory meals — something you enjoy and savor fully.
Move in joy — dance, flow, or stretch to honor your body's partnership in your progress.

Today I nourish my body with:

Today I move with intention through:

"Gratitude sustains my evolution."

EVENING GRATITUDE

Acknowledging growth helped me feel:

TRUEJOY-LIVING

A YEAR OF TRANSFORMATION

DAY 112-Expansion & Renewal — Living the Evolution

"I move from truth, not approval."

MORNING RITUAL

Sit quietly with a straight spine and soft heart. Take three slow breaths and ask yourself: "What feels aligned for me today?" Write or say your answer aloud — without considering what others expect. Whisper: "I honor my truth above all else." (This ritual trains intuitive decision-making and releases people-pleasing tendencies that block peace.)

JOURNAL REFLECTION

Where am I still acting from external expectation?
What does alignment feel like in my body?
What would happen if I trusted that more?

MEAL & MOVEMENT

Eat meals that make you feel clear and calm — not sluggish or pressured. Move in ways that feel natural today, not forced — your body knows the rhythm of alignment.

Today I nourish my body with:

Today I move with intention through:

"Alignment is my compass. Truth is my peace."

EVENING GRATITUDE

One choice I made from alignment today:

TRUEJOY-LIVING

A YEAR OF TRANSFORMATION

DAY 113-Expansion & Renewal — Living the Evolution

"I allow life to unfold with ease."

MORNING RITUAL

Take a deep breath and say softly: "I release the need to control."

Close your eyes and visualize a river flowing — steady, effortless, alive. See yourself floating on its surface, supported and guided, doing nothing but allowing.

(This ritual nurtures surrender — reminding you that allowing doesn't mean inaction, but trust.)

MEAL & MOVEMENT

Eat slowly — chew each bite fully and breathe between. Move in fluid, circular patterns — flow yoga, gentle dance, or mindful walking to embody ease.

Today I nourish my body with:

_____

Today I move with intention through:

_____

JOURNAL REFLECTION

What parts of my life am I still trying to control? How does allowing feel different than efforting? What blessings often come when I release resistance?

_____

"I allow life's grace to guide me."

EVENING GRATITUDE

Trusting flow helped me feel:

_____

_____

TRUEJOY-LIVING

A YEAR OF TRANSFORMATION

DAY 114-Expansion & Renewal —
Living the Evolution
"My presence is my greatest power."

MORNING RITUAL

Before checking messages or plans, take three mindful breaths.
Notice your surroundings — the light, the air, the texture of the
floor beneath you. Whisper: "I am fully here."
As you move into your morning, give your full attention to each
moment, task, and person — one at a time.
(This ritual grounds leadership and influence in mindfulness —
power comes from presence, not pressure.)

JOURNAL REFLECTION

How often am I truly present versus distracted?
What changes when I give full attention to what's in front of me?
How can I lead today through calm awareness instead of
urgency?

MEAL & MOVEMENT

Eat without screens — taste, savor, and breathe. Move with focus
— walk, stretch, or practice slow, deliberate motions that bring
awareness into every movement.

Today I nourish my body with:

Today I move with intention through:

"Presence is peace in action."

EVENING GRATITUDE

A moment of pure presence I experienced today:

DAY 115-Expansion & Renewal — Living the Evolution
"Joy is my natural frequency."

MORNING RITUAL

Upon waking, stretch and smile gently — even if you don't feel like it yet. Say aloud: "Today, I choose joy."
Write down one joyful act you'll gift yourself today — small or big — and commit to it.
(This ritual transforms joy from a mood into a mindful, daily choice.)

JOURNAL REFLECTION

What activities or people spark genuine joy for me?
How can I prioritize joy without guilt?
How does joy fuel my evolution?

MEAL & MOVEMENT

Eat foods that bring comfort and light — something colorful or nostalgic. Move in ways that feel fun and freeing — dance, sway, or walk to music you love.

Today I nourish my body with:

Today I move with intention through:

"Joy expands everything it touches — including me."

EVENING GRATITUDE

A joyful moment I created today:

DAY 116-Expansion & Renewal — Living the Evolution

"Peace is my practice, not my pursuit."

MORNING RITUAL

Sit still and take three deep breaths. Visualize your day ahead as a calm lake — still, reflective, unbothered by wind.

Whisper: "I bring peace wherever I go."

Throughout the day, pause before reacting — breathe, soften, and respond from that lake of calm.

(This ritual turns peace from a concept into a conscious daily behavior.)

JOURNAL REFLECTION

What actions or words helped me maintain peace today?

Where did I lose it, and what lesson can I take from that?

How can I become a living example of peace for others?

MEAL & MOVEMENT

Eat slowly and peacefully — avoid multitasking or rushing. Move gently and fluidly — focus on how each motion can calm your system.

Today I nourish my body with:

_____

Today I move with intention through:

_____

"Peace flows through everything I do."

EVENING GRATITUDE

A peaceful choice I made today:

_____

_____

DAY 117-Expansion & Renewal — Living the Evolution

"Grace carries me, and gratitude grounds me."

MORNING RITUAL

Take three slow breaths and whisper: "I move
through this day with grace."
Visualize yourself walking gently through your day
— calm, open-hearted, compassionate. Before you
rise, name three things you're grateful for, then
smile into your morning.
(This ritual integrates humility and reverence —
grace is movement guided by gratitude.)

_____

_____

JOURNAL REFLECTION

How can I respond with grace to life's
imperfections?
What am I most grateful for today?
How does grace shift my energy and relationships?

_____

_____

MEAL & MOVEMENT

Eat simply and mindfully, giving thanks for
nourishment. Move with elegance and intention —
yoga, stretching, or mindful walking.

Today I nourish my body with:

_____

Today I move with intention through:

_____

"Grace and gratitude light my path."

EVENING GRATITUDE
A moment I embodied grace today:

_____

_____

DAY 118-Expansion & Renewal —
Living the Evolution
"Stillness is where my wisdom speaks."

MORNING RITUAL

Find a quiet place to sit. Take three deep breaths and listen
— not for sound, but for silence.
Whisper softly: "I am at peace in the pause."
Allow stillness to fill your mind like light fills a room.
(This ritual reminds participants that strength grows in
still moments — evolution matures through rest and
reflection.)

MEAL & MOVEMENT

Eat in silence, noticing texture, scent, and flavor. Move
meditatively — slow walking or stretching with breath
awareness.

Today I nourish my body with:

Today I move with intention through:

JOURNAL REFLECTION

How does stillness feel in my body and mind?
What insights arise when I slow down?
How can I create more sacred pauses in my week?

*"Stillness restores me. Wisdom
blooms in quiet."*

EVENING GRATITUDE

A moment of stillness I cherished today:

DAY 119–Wholeness & Integration: The Evolution Embodied

"Every experience has shaped me into who I am becoming."

MORNING RITUAL

Take three slow breaths. Whisper: "Everything I've experienced has served my evolution."

Close your eyes and visualize your journey — the grounding, awakening, manifesting, and healing.

Feel gratitude for every step — the light, the challenge, the grace.

(This ritual unites your entire journey — integration turns experience into embodied wisdom.)

MEAL & MOVEMENT

Eat something nourishing and familiar — a meal that symbolizes comfort and completion. Move intuitively — let your body stretch, flow, or rest with gratitude.

Today I nourish my body with:

Today I move with intention through:

JOURNAL REFLECTION

What lessons or insights stand out most from my journey so far?

How have I changed in the way I think, feel, and choose?

What new truths guide my daily life now?

"I am whole. Every chapter has meaning."

EVENING GRATITUDE

One insight I embodied today:

DAY 120-Wholeness & Integration: The Evolution Embodied

"I trust the seasons of my soul."

MORNING RITUAL

Look outside — whether it's sunrise, rain, or clouds — and whisper:

"Just as nature evolves in cycles, so do I."

Take three deep breaths and imagine each inhale as renewal and each exhale as release.

Flow with your current season — whether blooming or resting.

(This ritual aligns inner evolution with nature's rhythm — a reminder that growth is cyclical, not linear.)

MEAL & MOVEMENT

at seasonally — foods fresh from your region. Move with nature — step outside, feel the air, let your breath match the earth's pace.

Today I nourish my body with:

_____

Today I move with intention through:

_____

"I trust the timing of my evolution."

JOURNAL REFLECTION

Which "season" am I in right now — planting, blooming, harvesting, or resting?

How can I support myself in this phase?

What does honoring my cycles look like in practice?

_____

_____

EVENING GRATITUDE

A rhythm or pattern I honored today:

_____

_____

DAY 121-Wholeness & Integration: The Evolution Embodied

"I see myself through the eyes of compassion and truth."

MORNING RITUAL

Stand before a mirror. Look into your own eyes —
softly, lovingly.

Whisper: "I see you. I love who you're becoming."

Notice not just your face, but your light — the
energy that shines through.

(This ritual transforms self-perception — seeing
yourself through truth, not judgment.)

MEAL & MOVEMENT

Eat meals that make you feel radiant — bright
fruits, greens, and hydration. Move with
awareness — mirror work, posture alignment, or
gentle movement that honors your reflection.

Today I nourish my body with:

_____

Today I move with intention through:

_____

JOURNAL REFLECTION

How do I see myself differently now than I did at the
start of this journey?

What qualities do I admire in who I am today?

How can I keep seeing myself through love instead of
criticism?

_____

_____

"I see my light clearly, and I honor it."

EVENING GRATITUDE

Something I appreciated about myself today:

_____

_____

TRUEJOY-LIVING

A YEAR OF TRANSFORMATION

DAY 122–Wholeness & Integration: The Evolution Embodied

"I am centered, calm, and whole."

MORNING RITUAL

Take a deep breath in through your nose, exhale through your mouth. Visualize balance between giving and receiving, effort and rest, doing and being.

Whisper: "I am balanced and steady within myself." (This ritual re-centers energy — equilibrium is the essence of evolution.)

MEAL & MOVEMENT

at a balanced meal — sweet and savory, light and grounding. Move evenly — pairing stillness with strength, flow with stability.

Today I nourish my body with:

_____

Today I move with intention through:

_____

JOURNAL REFLECTION

Where in my life am I leaning too far into effort or stillness?

What daily habits help me return to center?

How can I honor balance as an act of self-respect?

_____

_____

"Balance is my anchor and my freedom."

EVENING GRATITUDE

A moment I felt balanced today:

_____

_____

DAY 123-Wholeness & Integration:
The Evolution Embodied

"Nothing is missing; everything I need lives within me."

MORNING RITUAL

Sit quietly, breathe deeply, and place one hand over your heart and one over your belly. Feel the rhythm of your breath connecting both — unity in motion.
Whisper: "I am complete in this moment."
(This ritual solidifies inner wholeness — fullness is found within, not beyond.)

MEAL & MOVEMENT

Eat meals that feel complete yet light — balanced nourishment. Move slowly and fully — yoga, qigong, or stretching to embody connection.

Today I nourish my body with:

Today I move with intention through:

"I am already everything I've been seeking."

JOURNAL REFLECTION

What parts of me have I reintegrated through this journey?
How does wholeness feel in my mind, body, and heart?
How do I remind myself that I am already complete?

EVENING GRATITUDE

Remembering my completeness helped me feel:

DAY 124-Wholeness & Integration: The Evolution Embodied

"Truth flows through me effortlessly."

MORNING RITUAL

Take three slow breaths.
Say softly: "I speak and act in alignment with my truth."
Visualize your day unfolding naturally — every word, decision, and action flowing from authenticity.
(This ritual merges honesty with harmony — truth as ease, not effort.)

MEAL & MOVEMENT

Eat mindfully, listening to what your body truly needs. Move gracefully — slow, open, intentional.

Today I nourish my body with:

_____

Today I move with intention through:

_____

JOURNAL REFLECTION

What does "living my truth" mean to me now?
How can I express authenticity with grace, not force?
What does it feel like when I'm fully aligned with my truth?

_____

_____

"Truth flows freely through all I do."

EVENING GRATITUDE

A moment of authentic living today:

_____

_____

DAY 125-Wholeness & Integration: The Evolution Embodied

"I am the flow of evolution — grounded, grateful, and free."

MORNING RITUAL

Stand tall, take a deep breath, and smile softly.
Whisper: "I evolve with life, not against it."
Visualize yourself as a river — clear, strong, adaptable, endlessly moving forward.
(This ritual celebrates unity with the greater rhythm — the soul's evolution is never-ending, yet always whole.)

JOURNAL REFLECTION

How has my relationship with change transformed?
How can I remain adaptable while grounded in truth?
What does living in harmony with life mean for me now?

MEAL & MOVEMENT

Eat what feels alive and balanced — fruits, grains, greens, and warmth. Move naturally — a walk, dance, or stretch that connects you to life's pulse.

Today I nourish my body with:

_____

Today I move with intention through:

_____

"I evolve with grace, always becoming, always whole."

EVENING GRATITUDE

One moment I felt harmony with life today:

_____

_____

DAY 126–Courage & Confidence

"My power is peaceful, purposeful, and kind."

MORNING RITUAL

Stand tall with feet hip-width apart. Take three slow breaths, feeling your spine lengthen. Whisper: "I call my energy back to me." Visualize golden light rising from your feet to your crown — reclaiming every piece of yourself once given away to fear, doubt, or over-giving.
(This ritual activates sovereignty — power rooted in peace, not force.)

JOURNAL REFLECTION

Where have I been giving my power away?
What does "peaceful strength" look like for me?
How will I choose empowered energy today?

MEAL & MOVEMENT

Eat grounding yet energizing foods — grains, root veggies, seeds. Move strongly — power walking, steady yoga, or standing poses that awaken strength.

Today I nourish my body with:

_____

Today I move with intention through:

_____

"My power is my peace."

EVENING GRATITUDE

A moment I stood in my power today:

_____

_____

DAY 127-Courage & Confidence

"Courage is my compass."

MORNING RITUAL

Take three breaths.
On each inhale, whisper: "I am brave."
On each exhale: "I release fear."
Visualize stepping beyond a familiar doorway — light on
the other side calling you forward.
(This ritual reminds you courage isn't the absence of fear,
but movement through it.)

JOURNAL REFLECTION

Where can I choose courage instead of comfort today?
What past moment proved I'm stronger than fear?
What does brave action look like right now?

MEAL & MOVEMENT

Eat clean and energizing meals — citrus, greens, water.
Move boldly — try something new, challenge your body
safely, or take a brisk walk with upbeat music.

Today I nourish my body with:

Today I move with intention through:

"Courage opens every door I walk through."

EVENING GRATITUDE

One courageous act I took today:

DAY 128-Courage & Confidence

"My voice is clear, confident, and compassionate."

MORNING RITUAL

Place a hand over your throat and breathe deeply.
Whisper:
"It's safe to speak my truth."
Hum softly or recite your favorite mantra aloud —
feel the vibration awakening your voice center.
(This ritual activates expression — truth spoken
with calm confidence.)

JOURNAL REFLECTION

What truths have I silenced and why?
How can I share honestly while remaining kind?
What does my authentic voice sound like?

MEAL & MOVEMENT

Sip warm teas to open the throat — ginger, honey,
lemon. Move with focus on posture and breath,
expanding chest and shoulders.

Today I nourish my body with:

Today I move with intention through:

"My voice carries wisdom and love."

EVENING GRATITUDE

Something I expressed with truth today:

TRUEJOY-LIVING

A YEAR OF TRANSFORMATION

DAY 129-Courage & Confidence

"Focused intention fuels empowered action."

MORNING RITUAL

Write one clear intention for the day — simple and meaningful.
Place your hand over it and whisper:
"I commit to this with focus and faith."
(This ritual transforms intention into embodied direction — discipline as devotion.)

JOURNAL REFLECTION

What one goal or promise matters most today?
How can I show up for it fully?
What does consistency feel like in my body?

MEAL & MOVEMENT

Eat steady, sustaining meals — protein, grains, water. Move with structure — a planned walk, timed yoga flow, or posture practice.

Today I nourish my body with:

Today I move with intention through:

"My consistency builds my confidence."

EVENING GRATITUDE

One intention I honored today:

DAY 130-Courage & Confidence

"Every challenge strengthens my spirit."

MORNING RITUAL

Take three deep breaths and whisper:
"I welcome growth in all forms."
Visualize yourself climbing a gentle hill — each step
representing learning, resilience, and grace.
(This ritual reframes obstacles as opportunities —
every test is a teacher.)

MEAL & MOVEMENT

Eat grounding foods — beans, grains, hearty soups.
Move with endurance — steady cardio or long walks
to build stamina

Today I nourish my body with:

_____

Today I move with intention through:

_____

JOURNAL REFLECTION

What current challenge might be teaching me?
How can I meet it with curiosity instead of frustration?
What strength is emerging through this process?

_____

"Challenges refine me into my highest self."

EVENING GRATITUDE
A challenge I faced with grace today:

_____

DAY 131–Courage & Confidence

"My leadership uplifts others through love."

MORNING RITUAL

Sit tall, hand on heart, and whisper:
"I lead by example, not by control."
Visualize yourself radiating calm influence —
empowering others through presence and
understanding.
(This ritual embodies conscious leadership — firm
but kind.)

JOURNAL REFLECTION

How can I lead with empathy instead of ego?
Who in my life benefits when I stand in calm
authority?
What does heart-centered leadership mean to me?

MEAL & MOVEMENT

Eat shared meals if possible — connection
nourishes leadership. Move in teamwork — group
yoga, family walk, or collaborative activity.

Today I nourish my body with:

Today I move with intention through:

"My leadership is rooted in love."

EVENING GRATITUDE

Compassionate confidence helped me feel:

DAY 132-Courage & Confidence

"I am strong, steady, and proud of who I'm becoming."

MORNING RITUAL

Place a hand on your heart and whisper:
"I honor my strength — past, present, and future."
Smile at your reflection or write down three
qualities that make you resilient.

JOURNAL REFLECTION

What inner strengths have carried me this far?

How do I define true strength now?

How can I honor my resilience daily?

MEAL & MOVEMENT

Eat foods that feel empowering — rich in color and
flavor. Move expressively — dance, power poses, or
movement that celebrates vitality.

Today I nourish my body with:

Today I move with intention through:

"Strength and grace live within me always."

EVENING GRATITUDE

Acknowledging power helped me feel:

DAY 133-Boundaries, Discipline & Integrity

"Boundaries protect my peace, not my walls."

MORNING RITUAL

Close your eyes and take three deep breaths.
Visualize a soft, golden light encircling you —
permeable enough for love, firm enough for peace.
Whisper: "I choose where my energy flows today."
(This ritual restores energetic sovereignty — love
and limits can coexist beautifully.)

_____

_____

JOURNAL REFLECTION

Where do I most need to reinforce a loving
boundary?
What does saying "no" make space for?
How can I express boundaries calmly and clearly?

_____

_____

MEAL & MOVEMENT

Eat grounding meals — roasted roots, grains, warm
tea. Move intentionally — slow standing poses or a
deliberate walk that reinforces stability.

Today I nourish my body with:

_____

Today I move with intention through:

_____

"Boundaries are acts of self-respect."

EVENING GRATITUDE

Protecting my peace helped me feel:

_____

_____

DAY 134-Boundaries, Discipline & Integrity

"Discipline is devotion to my highest self."

MORNING RITUAL

Write one simple commitment for today and say aloud:

"I honor my word with action."

Breathe into your solar plexus, feeling warmth ignite focus and purpose.

(This ritual reframes discipline as sacred follow-through rather than rigid control.)

MEAL & MOVEMENT

Eat balanced, energizing meals — steady fuel. Move consistently — even ten mindful minutes count; consistency matters more than intensity.

Today I nourish my body with:

Today I move with intention through:

JOURNAL REFLECTION

What helps me keep promises to myself?

Where does discipline become harsh instead of devoted?

How can I make consistency feel sacred?

"Every small act of devotion strengthens my integrity."

EVENING GRATITUDE

Showing up for myself helped me feel:

DAY 135-Boundaries, Discipline & Integrity

"My actions reflect my truth."

MORNING RITUAL

Place a hand over your heart and whisper:
"May everything I do today be aligned with who I am."
Visualize your words, choices, and energy forming one bright line of honesty.
(This ritual merges intention with integrity — harmony between inner and outer worlds.)

MEAL & MOVEMENT

Eat clean, simple meals — nothing hidden or excessive. Move consciously — posture aligned, breath steady; each motion mirrors inner clarity.

Today I nourish my body with:

Today I move with intention through:

JOURNAL REFLECTION

Where do my actions already reflect my values?
Where might I be out of alignment?
How can I course-correct gently?

"Integrity is my quiet strength."

EVENING GRATITUDE

Alignment helped me feel:

DAY 136-Boundaries, Discipline & Integrity

"My energy is sacred currency."

MORNING RITUAL

List three things that truly deserve your energy today.
Say aloud: "I spend my energy with intention."
(This ritual invites energetic budgeting — choosing focus that nourishes instead of depletes.)

_____

_____

JOURNAL REFLECTION

What energizes me? What drains me?
How can I protect my vitality during the day?
What one boundary will preserve my energy tomorrow?

_____

_____

MEAL & MOVEMENT

Eat steady-fuel meals — protein, hydration, greens. Move to recharge — breathing breaks, short walks, or stretching every few hours.

Today I nourish my body with:

_____

Today I move with intention through:

_____

"I invest my energy where it grows love and purpose."

EVENING GRATITUDE

Conserving energy helped me feel:

_____

_____

DAY 137-Boundaries, Discipline & Integrity

"Accountability strengthens my trust in myself.

MORNING RITUAL

Look at your reflection or journal and whisper:

"I take responsibility with compassion."

(This ritual transforms accountability from blame to empowerment.)

MEAL & MOVEMENT

Eat clean, clarifying meals — greens, citrus. Move mindfully — posture-based or balancing exercises to embody self-support.

Today I nourish my body with:

_____

Today I move with intention through:

_____

JOURNAL REFLECTION

What am I ready to take ownership of today?
How can I learn from mistakes without shame?
What accountability practice builds self-trust?

_____

_____

"Accountability is self-respect in action."

EVENING GRATITUDE

Honest ownership helped me feel:

_____

_____

DAY 138-Boundaries, Discipline & Integrity

"Focused energy creates freedom."

MORNING RITUAL

Before beginning tasks, close your eyes and whisper:
"One thing at a time."
Visualize your mind as a calm lake — ripples of distraction settle into clarity.
(This ritual reinforces mindful productivity — focus as peace, not pressure.)

_____

_____

JOURNAL REFLECTION

What distractions often pull me away from purpose?
How does focus feel compared to multitasking?
What boundaries support my concentration?

_____

_____

MEAL & MOVEMENT

Eat light meals to maintain alertness — fresh veggies, hydration. Move intentionally — brief focus walks or stretches between tasks.

Today I nourish my body with:

_____

Today I move with intention through:

_____

"Focused presence is my superpower."

EVENING GRATITUDE

Clarity helped me feel:

_____

_____

DAY 139-Boundaries, Discipline & Integrity

"Rest restores my power."

MORNING RITUAL

Upon waking, take three unhurried breaths.
Say softly:
"I am allowed to rest."
(This ritual honors recovery as the foundation of sustainable power.)

MEAL & MOVEMENT

Eat soothing, replenishing meals — soups, teas. Move gently — stretching, restorative yoga, or simply stillness.

Today I nourish my body with:

_____

Today I move with intention through:

_____

JOURNAL REFLECTION

How do I feel when I truly rest without guilt?
What stops me from slowing down?
How can I make rest part of my daily rhythm?

_____

"Rest is power. I am restored."

EVENING GRATITUDE

A moment of rest I honored today:

_____

_____

TRUEJOY-LIVING

A YEAR OF TRANSFORMATION

DAY 140-Courageous Action & Authentic Leadership
"Aligned action turns vision into reality."

MORNING RITUAL

Place a hand over your heart and whisper: "Today I move with purpose."
Visualize your most important intention surrounded by golden light. See yourself taking one bold, clear step toward it.
(This ritual activates momentum rooted in alignment — courage in motion.)

_____

_____

MEAL & MOVEMENT

Eat energizing meals — protein, fresh greens, hydration. Move with vigor — brisk walking, power yoga, or an action that awakens confidence.

Today I nourish my body with:

_____

Today I move with intention through:

_____

JOURNAL REFLECTION

What bold action is calling me today?
How can I move forward without waiting for perfect timing?
What does "aligned action" feel like in my body?

_____

_____

"Courage and clarity guide my every step."

EVENING GRATITUDE

One action I took with courage today:

_____

_____

DAY 141-Courageous Action & Authentic Leadership

"My actions inspire others to rise."

MORNING RITUAL

Take a deep breath and whisper: "I am a living example of love in action."

As you move through the morning, imagine others feeling uplifted simply by your calm, grounded presence.

(This ritual anchors authentic leadership — influence through embodiment, not instruction.)

JOURNAL REFLECTION

Who or what do I lead through my presence?
What qualities make me a leader others can trust?
How can I live those qualities today?

MEAL & MOVEMENT

Eat balanced, shared meals if possible — community strengthens leadership. Move with poise — yoga, dance, or any practice that refines posture and grace.

Today I nourish my body with:

_____

Today I move with intention through:

_____

"My presence leads with love."

EVENING GRATITUDE

Leading authentically helped me feel:

_____

_____

DAY 142–Courageous Action & Authentic Leadership

"My voice is a vessel of clarity and courage."

MORNING RITUAL

Before beginning your day, place a hand on your throat and breathe deeply.
Whisper: "My words create light."
Speak one empowering truth aloud — something you've been holding inside — even if only to yourself.

JOURNAL REFLECTION

What truth do I need to express today?
How can I communicate it clearly and compassionately?
What happens when I stop silencing my truth?

MEAL & MOVEMENT

Eat soothing, warming meals — teas with honey, soups. Move through expressive flow — stretches, singing, or even reading aloud with confidence.

Today I nourish my body with:

_____

Today I move with intention through:

_____

"My voice is clear, confident, and kind."

EVENING GRATITUDE

Speaking from courage helped me feel:

_____

_____

DAY 143–Courageous Action & Authentic Leadership

"Fear shows me where I am ready to grow."

MORNING RITUAL

Close your eyes and take a deep breath. Name one fear aloud. Then whisper: "Thank you for showing me where courage begins."

Visualize that fear dissolving into light — transforming into strength that propels you forward.

(This ritual reframes fear as guidance, not opposition.)

MEAL & MOVEMENT

Eat grounding meals — root veggies, proteins, herbal teas. Move dynamically — walks, runs, or strength work to transmute fear into energy.

Today I nourish my body with:

Today I move with intention through:

JOURNAL REFLECTION

What fear has been guiding my choices?
How can I meet it with curiosity instead of avoidance?
What lesson or energy does this fear hold?

"Fear is energy returning to power."

EVENING GRATITUDE

Reframing fear helped me feel:

TRUEJOY-LIVING

A YEAR OF TRANSFORMATION

DAY 144–Courageous Action & Authentic Leadership

"My strength uplifts those around me."

MORNING RITUAL

Take a deep breath and whisper: "May my energy be a blessing wherever I go."
Visualize a warm light expanding from your heart, touching others with love, confidence, and encouragement.
(This ritual redefines leadership as energetic generosity.)

MEAL & MOVEMENT

Eat shared or family-style meals if possible — connection feeds community. Move socially — walk with someone, teach, or share a joyful practice.

Today I nourish my body with:

Today I move with intention through:

JOURNAL REFLECTION

Who can I uplift today through encouragement or kindness?
How does sharing my light enhance my own growth?
What does empowerment mean beyond myself?

"The more I give, the more light flows through me."

EVENING GRATITUDE

Sharing my strength helped me feel:

DAY 145–Courageous Action &
Authentic Leadership
"True strength is steady, not loud."

MORNING RITUAL

Stand tall, barefoot if possible. Take three slow breaths, feeling the ground beneath you.
Whisper:
"I root my power in peace."
(This ritual blends confidence with humility — power stabilized by calm awareness.)

MEAL & MOVEMENT

Eat nourishing, earthy meals — whole grains, beans, teas. Move with awareness — grounding yoga or slow, mindful walks.

Today I nourish my body with:

Today I move with intention through:

JOURNAL REFLECTION

When do I feel most grounded in my strength?
What knocks me off center, and how can I stay steady?
How does grounded confidence differ from ego-driven power?

"Grounded power is my natural state."

EVENING GRATITUDE

Calm strength helped me feel:

TRUEJOY-LIVING
A YEAR OF TRANSFORMATION

DAY 146–Courageous Action & Authentic Leadership

"Leadership is love in motion."

MORNING RITUAL

Take three deep breaths and whisper:
"May everything I do today uplift the greater good."
Visualize your energy flowing outward — each action a ripple of positive impact.
(This ritual celebrates service-led leadership — influence through intention and contribution.)

JOURNAL REFLECTION

How can I serve from love, not obligation?
What legacy do I want to leave through my leadership?
How can I uplift others while staying true to my own balance?

MEAL & MOVEMENT

Eat generous, wholesome meals — nourishing yourself as you nourish others. Move in community — group walks, volunteer activities, or shared practices.

Today I nourish my body with:

Today I move with intention through:

"Service amplifies my purpose."

EVENING GRATITUDE

One way I served with love today:

DAY 147-Resilience, Mastery & Emotional Strength

"Change is not chaos — it is transformation in motion."

MORNING RITUAL

Sit quietly and take three grounding breaths.
Whisper: "I am safe as life shifts around me."
Visualize yourself as the calm center of a spinning wheel — still, steady, unshaken — as the outer world moves naturally.
(This ritual stabilizes emotional energy during uncertain or transitional times.)

JOURNAL REFLECTION

How do I usually respond to unexpected change?
What helps me stay calm and grounded?
What wisdom is this current change bringing me?

MEAL & MOVEMENT

Eat comforting but clean meals — soups, grains, herbal teas. Move slowly — gentle flow or deep-breath walking to stay centered.

Today I nourish my body with:

_____

Today I move with intention through:

_____

"I am the calm within the current."

EVENING GRATITUDE

A moment I stayed calm in change today:

_____

_____

TRUEJOY-LIVING

A YEAR OF TRANSFORMATION

DAY 148-Resilience, Mastery & Emotional Strength

"What I resist, I invite with love to transform."

MORNING RITUAL

Take a slow, deep breath. Visualize resistance as a
tight knot in your chest or mind — then breathe
light into it until it softens and opens.
 Whisper: "I release resistance and move with
grace."
(This ritual turns friction into flow — energy
released becomes strength restored.)

_____

_____

JOURNAL REFLECTION

What am I resisting right now and why?
How might acceptance ease this experience?
What gifts could emerge from surrender?

_____

_____

MEAL & MOVEMENT

Eat hydrating, cleansing meals — fruits,
greens, lemon water. Move fluidly — dance,
stretch, or gentle shaking to release tension.

 Today I nourish my body with:

_____

Today I move with intention through:

_____

"Flow restores my freedom"

EVENING GRATITUDE
Allowing flow helped me feel:

_____

_____

DAY 149-Resilience, Mastery & Emotional Strength

"Faith anchors me when the path is unclear."

MORNING RITUAL

Close your eyes, place your hand over your heart, and whisper: "I trust the unfolding."
Visualize yourself walking through fog — each step revealing just enough light to continue forward.
(This ritual strengthens trust when clarity is limited — faith as the steady bridge between the known and unknown.)

MEAL & MOVEMENT

Eat soothing, simple foods — oatmeal, warm grains, teas. Move with intention — slow walking or prayerful movement.

Today I nourish my body with:

_____

Today I move with intention through:

_____

JOURNAL REFLECTION

What uncertainty am I learning to trust right now?
How has faith carried me in the past?
How can I nurture faith daily through action?

"Faith is my quiet confidence."

EVENING GRATITUDE

Trusting the process helped me feel:

_____

DAY 150-Resilience, Mastery & Emotional Strength

"I master emotions by listening, not reacting."

MORNING RITUAL

Take three conscious breaths.
Whisper: "I respond from understanding, not reaction."
Throughout the day, when emotion arises, pause and breathe before responding — letting wisdom, not impulse, speak.
(This ritual trains emotional intelligence — presence as mastery.)

MEAL & MOVEMENT

Eat steady, balanced meals — grounding foods to regulate mood. Move with mindfulness — slow yoga or deep-breath walks.

Today I nourish my body with:

_____

Today I move with intention through:

_____

JOURNAL REFLECTION

What emotion challenged me most today?
How did I respond, and what did I learn?
What supports me in staying balanced emotionally?

"Emotional wisdom is my strength."

EVENING GRATITUDE

Responding mindfully helped me feel:

_____

_____

DAY 151-Resilience, Mastery & Emotional Strength

"I rise stronger each time I fall."

MORNING RITUAL

Stand tall, take three deep breaths, and whisper:
"I am resilient by nature."
Visualize a seed sprouting through soil — gentle, persistent, unstoppable.
(This ritual rewires the nervous system for resilience — grace under pressure.)

MEAL & MOVEMENT

Eat energizing meals — hearty grains, protein, citrus. Move with vigor — cardio, power poses, or grounding stretches.

Today I nourish my body with:

_____

Today I move with intention through:

_____

JOURNAL REFLECTION

How do I usually handle setbacks?
What helps me rebound faster?
What proof do I have that I always find my way back?

_____

"Every fall refines my strength"

EVENING GRATITUDE

Rising again helped me feel:

_____

_____

TRUEJOY-LIVING

A YEAR OF TRANSFORMATION

DAY 152-Resilience, Mastery & Emotional Strength
"My sensitivity amplifies my strength."

MORNING RITUAL

Take a deep breath, hand on heart.
Whisper: "My sensitivity is wisdom, not weakness."
(This ritual harmonizes emotional intelligence and courage — both are needed for true leadership.)

MEAL & MOVEMENT

Eat nurturing meals — soups, fruits, herbal teas.
Move gently — intuitive yoga, slow dance, or mindful breathing.

Today I nourish my body with:

_____

Today I move with intention through:

_____

JOURNAL REFLECTION

How does my sensitivity enhance my leadership?
When have I mistaken it for weakness?
How can I use empathy as strength today?

"Softness and strength coexist within me."

EVENING GRATITUDE
Compassionate strength helped me feel:

_____

_____

DAY 153-Resilience, Mastery &
Emotional Strength
"No matter what comes. I rise in grace."

MORNING RITUAL

Close your eyes and breathe deeply. Whisper:
"I have overcome before, and I can again."
Visualize every challenge you've moved through —
feel gratitude for your own endurance and grace.
(This ritual completes the resilience cycle — trust
built through evidence of strength.)

MEAL & MOVEMENT

Eat foods that renew — colorful vegetables,
grains, clean water. Move with flow — brisk
walking or stretching that embodies
confidence.

Today I nourish my body with:

_____

Today I move with intention through:

_____

JOURNAL REFLECTION

What moments have proven my resilience?
How can I remind myself of this strength in the
future?
What does "grace under fire" look like for me?

"Resilience is my natural rhythm."

EVENING GRATITUDE

Trusting myself helped me feel:

_____

DAY 154-Purposeful Power & Legacy—
Living Empowered
"Every action I take carries purpose."

MORNING RITUAL

Take three deep breaths and whisper: "May everything I do today align with my purpose."
Pause before beginning any task and ask: "Does this serve my growth or my peace?"
(This ritual centers each day in intention, helping align purpose with presence.)

MEAL & MOVEMENT

Eat with awareness — whole, nourishing foods. Move mindfully — yoga, walking, or stretching with a focus on gratitude for your body.

Today I nourish my body with:

_____

Today I move with intention through:

_____

JOURNAL REFLECTION

What does living "on purpose" mean for me?
How can I bring more intention into ordinary actions?
What am I here to create, share, or embody?

_____

_____

"Purpose flows through everything I do."

EVENING GRATITUDE

Living intentionally helped me feel:

_____

_____

DAY 155-Purposeful Power & Legacy—
Living Empowered
"My authenticity invites others to be real."

MORNING RITUAL

Stand before a mirror and take a deep breath.
Smile gently and whisper: "My truth is my gift."
Throughout the day, practice honesty — not
perfection — in words, presence, and energy.
(This ritual builds influence rooted in truth —
authentic energy radiates naturally.)

MEAL & MOVEMENT

Eat what feels most authentic to your body's
needs. Move expressively — stretch, dance,
or walk in ways that honor your uniqueness.

Today I nourish my body with:

_____

Today I move with intention through:

_____

JOURNAL REFLECTION

When do I feel most authentic?
What holds me back from being fully seen?
How can my authenticity serve others today?

_____

_____

"Authenticity is my superpower."

EVENING GRATITUDE

A moment I showed up authentically today:

_____

_____

DAY 156-Purposeful Power & Legacy—Living Empowered
"My light helps others find their own."

MORNING RITUAL

Take a deep breath and whisper: "May my energy uplift everyone I meet." Visualize your heart expanding — each breath radiating light that gently awakens the potential in others.

(This ritual turns empowerment outward — the essence of purpose-driven leadership.)

MEAL & MOVEMENT

Eat communal or shared meals — food made with love nourishes connection. Move in partnership — group walks, classes, or mindful teamwork.

Today I nourish my body with:

_____

Today I move with intention through:

_____

JOURNAL REFLECTION

Who in my life could use encouragement or guidance today?

How can I empower without rescuing?

What does shared growth look like to me?

_____

_____

> *"My light grows brighter when shared."*

EVENING GRATITUDE

Empowering others helped me feel:

_____

_____

DAY 157—Purposeful Power & Legacy—Living Empowered

"My vision is guided by love."

MORNING RITUAL

Sit quietly, hand over heart. Whisper: "Show me what's possible through love today."
Imagine your life five years from now — led by compassion, not fear. See yourself guiding others gently into their greatness.
(This ritual activates visionary leadership — purpose connected to compassion.)

JOURNAL REFLECTION

What is my long-term vision rooted in love?
How do I lead from heart, not ego?
What first step toward that vision can I take today?

MEAL & MOVEMENT

Eat light and energizing meals — fruit, grains, fresh air. Move fluidly — flow yoga or mindful walking while visualizing your next chapter.

Today I nourish my body with:

_____

Today I move with intention through:

_____

"My heart is my compass."

EVENING GRATITUDE

Leading with heart helped me feel:

_____

_____

DAY 158-Purposeful Power & Legacy—Living Empowered

"Power is sacred when guided by integrity."

MORNING RITUAL

Take three grounding breaths. Whisper: "I use my influence to create good."
Visualize your energy as a torch — bright, strong, steady — lighting paths without burning out yourself or others.
(This ritual reinforces humility in leadership — strength anchored in service.)

MEAL & MOVEMENT

Eat grounding, stable meals — rice, lentils, teas. Move slowly — balancing poses or mindful walks to stay centered.

Today I nourish my body with:

Today I move with intention through:

JOURNAL REFLECTION

Where do I hold influence in my life?
How can I use that power with compassion and fairness?
What values guide my leadership?

"My power serves the greater good."

EVENING GRATITUDE
Acting with integrity helped me feel:

DAY 159-Purposeful Power & Legacy—
Living Empowered
"My daily actions create my legacy."

MORNING RITUAL

Take three breaths and whisper:"The way I live today shapes tomorrow."
Write one word that reflects the energy you want to leave behind — love, courage, peace, joy — and carry it through your day.
(This ritual turns legacy into a living practice — how we show up now matters most.)

_____

_____

JOURNAL REFLECTION

How do I want people to feel in my presence?
What does living my legacy look like in everyday life?
What small action today reflects that legacy?

_____

_____

MEAL & MOVEMENT

Eat meals made with love — nourish yourself as you would a future self. Move intentionally — walk or stretch while repeating your chosen legacy word.

Today I nourish my body with:

_____

Today I move with intention through:

_____

_____

> *"My legacy is alive in how I love."*

EVENING GRATITUDE
Living with intention helped me feel:

_____

_____

DAY 160-Purposeful Power & Legacy— Living Empowered

"I am proud of who I've become."

MORNING RITUAL

Place both hands over your heart and whisper.
"Thank you, life, for shaping me into this version of myself."
Take a moment to reflect on how far you've come — from grounding to awakening, from healing to empowerment. Smile softly.

JOURNAL REFLECTION

What am I most proud of in my transformation so far?
How do I embody empowerment daily now?
What message would I share with my past self today?

MEAL & MOVEMENT

Eat celebratory, nourishing foods — something that feels like self-appreciation. Move joyfully — dance, walk, or stretch to honor your body's partnership.

Today I nourish my body with:

Today I move with intention through:

> *"Empowerment is my natural state."*

EVENING GRATITUDE

Honoring my journey helped me feel:

TRUEJOY-LIVING

A YEAR OF TRANSFORMATION

DAY 161-Presence, Integration & Self-Awareness

"My transformation is not a destination — it's how I live each day."

MORNING RITUAL

Take three slow breaths and whisper: "Today, I live from wisdom, not habit."

As you go about your morning, notice moments where you apply something you've learned — compassion, grounding, breath, awareness. Each one is integration in action.

(This ritual bridges reflection and embodiment — showing that growth happens through repetition of alignment.)

JOURNAL REFLECTION

What wisdom do I practice naturally now?

Where do I still fall back into old patterns?

What would living my transformation fully look like today?

MEAL & MOVEMENT

Eat intuitively, listening to your body's needs. Move in a way that reflects balance — grounding yoga, gentle walk, or dance flow.

Today I nourish my body with:

Today I move with intention through:

"I am becoming who I've always been."

EVENING GRATITUDE

Embodying growth helped me feel:

DAY 162-Presence, Integration & Self-Awareness

"Awareness is my anchor to the present."

MORNING RITUAL

Before moving from bed, place your hand on your heart and whisper: "I begin my day with awareness."
Notice the sensations — your breath, heartbeat, the sound of morning. Carry this attention with you into your first conversation, sip of water, or step outside.
(This ritual trains mindfulness as a way of being — awareness creates freedom.)

JOURNAL REFLECTION

How often do I move through my day on autopilot?
What helps me return to presence quickly?
How does awareness change the quality of my experiences?

MEAL & MOVEMENT

Eat with awareness — no distractions.
Move consciously — focusing on breath and muscle connection.

Today I nourish my body with:

Today I move with intention through:

"Awareness transforms everything it touches."

EVENING GRATITUDE

Awareness helped me feel:

DAY 163-Presence, Integration & Self-Awareness

"My body is the temple through which my soul expresses life."

MORNING RITUAL

Stand before a mirror or place your hands on your body with gratitude.

Whisper: "Thank you, body, for carrying me with love."

Stretch, breathe, and move slowly, feeling every muscle awaken.

(This ritual restores body reverence — embodiment as devotion.)

_____

_____

_____

JOURNAL REFLECTION

How have I spoken to or treated my body this week?

What does honoring my body look like?

What signals has my body been giving me lately?

_____

_____

MEAL & MOVEMENT

Eat whole, nourishing foods; hydrate deeply. Move lovingly — stretch, self-massage, or intuitive movement.

Today I nourish my body with:

_____

Today I move with intention through:

_____

"My body and spirit thrive in harmony."

EVENING GRATITUDE

Gratitude for my body helped me feel:

_____

_____

DAY 164-Presence, Integration & Self-Awareness

"Alignment is integrity in motion."

MORNING RITUAL

Write down one intention for your thoughts, one for your words, and one for your actions today. Whisper: "I live in harmony with what I believe." (This ritual refines coherence — inner alignment reflected outward.)

MEAL & MOVEMENT

Eat clearly and cleanly — minimal distractions, maximal nourishment. Move with purpose — walking or yoga centered on breath awareness.

Today I nourish my body with:

Today I move with intention through:

JOURNAL REFLECTION

Where am I most aligned in life right now? Where can I bring my actions closer to my values? How does alignment feel physically and emotionally?

"My life is my message."

EVENING GRATITUDE

Harmony helped me feel:

DAY 165-Presence, Integration & Self-Awareness

"I move through life with softness and strength."

MORNING RITUAL

Take a slow breath, smile gently, and whisper:
"Today, I choose ease."
As you move through your day, pause whenever
tension arises. Breathe deeply and imagine grace
flowing through every cell.
(This ritual helps participants embody peace in
motion — calm, not control.)

JOURNAL REFLECTION

Where in my life do I over-effort?
What does "ease" feel like in my body?
How can I bring grace to small daily moments?

MEAL & MOVEMENT

Eat light, fluid meals; drink herbal tea or
water. Move gracefully — slow walking,
flowing yoga, or mindful dancing.

Today I nourish my body with:

_____

Today I move with intention through:

_____

"Grace flows through me effortlessly."

EVENING GRATITUDE

Grace helped me feel:

_____

_____

DAY 166-Presence, Integration & Self-Awareness

"Stillness reveals what motion hides."

MORNING RITUAL

Find a quiet spot and take three slow breaths.
Whisper: "I am at peace in stillness."
Spend three minutes simply observing your breath
— doing nothing, fixing nothing, just being.
(This ritual teaches that silence and pause are
where guidance emerges.)

_____

_____

JOURNAL REFLECTION

How do I feel when I pause without distraction?
What messages arise in silence?
How can I create more still moments in my day?

_____

_____

MEAL & MOVEMENT

Eat in silence or with soft music; savor every bite.
Move gently — yin yoga, restorative stretches, or
deep breathing.

Today I nourish my body with:

_____

Today I move with intention through:

_____

"Stillness is my sacred teacher."

EVENING GRATITUDE

Stillness helped me feel:

_____

_____

DAY 167-Presence, Integration & Self-Awareness
"Peace begins with me and expands outward."

MORNING RITUAL

Take three breaths and visualize a circle of light around your body.
Whisper: "I carry peace wherever I go."
Throughout the day, notice how your presence affects spaces — practice being the calm in every interaction.
(This ritual is embodiment in action — peace practiced through presence.)

JOURNAL REFLECTION

How did I cultivate peace within myself today?
How did my peace influence others?
What disrupts my calm, and how can I return to it faster?

MEAL & MOVEMENT

Eat gently and slowly — meals that calm and comfort.
Move with awareness — peaceful yoga, slow walk, or breath practice.

Today I nourish my body with:

_____

Today I move with intention through:

_____

"I am peace embodied."

EVENING GRATITUDE
Living from calm helped me feel:

_____

TRUEJOY-LIVING
A YEAR OF TRANSFORMATION

DAY 168-Joyful Embodiment & Radiance — Living from Love, Pleasure, and Vitality

"Joy is my natural vibration."

MORNING RITUAL

As you wake, stretch your body and whisper: "I am grateful to feel alive."

Before your first sip of water or tea, smile intentionally — not because of anything external, but simply because you can.

(This ritual reawakens the heart — joy as a conscious state, not a fleeting mood.)

MEAL & MOVEMENT

Eat vibrant, colorful meals — fruits, greens, foods that feel alive. Move freely — dance, stretch, or walk with music that makes you smile.

Today I nourish my body with:

Today I move with intention through:

JOURNAL REFLECTION

What simple things bring me joy right now?

How can I weave play or lightness into my day?

How does joy shift my energy and creativity?

"Joy expands everything I touch."

EVENING GRATITUDE

Choosing happiness helped me feel:

DAY 169-Joyful Embodiment & Radiance — Living from Love, Pleasure, and Vitality

"Love flows through me effortlessly."

MORNING RITUAL

Place a hand over your heart and take three breaths.
Whisper: "May everything I do today be infused with love."
Imagine your heart glowing with golden light, expanding outward with each breath.
(This ritual shifts the body into heart coherence — radiance born from compassion.)

MEAL & MOVEMENT

Eat heart-nourishing meals — berries, greens, cacao. Move gently — heart-opening yoga, chest stretches, or breathing with soft music.

Today I nourish my body with:

_____

Today I move with intention through:

_____

JOURNAL REFLECTION

What does living from love look like for me?
How do I treat myself when I act from love?
How does love change the way I move through the world?

_____

_____

"I am love in motion."

EVENING GRATITUDE

Living from love helped me feel:

_____

_____

DAY 170-Joyful Embodiment & Radiance —
Living from Love, Pleasure, and Vitality
"My body is a living celebration of life."

MORNING RITUAL

Stand in front of a mirror or open space.
Move or stretch freely, feeling the energy awaken
within you. Whisper: "I celebrate the miracle of
being alive."
(This ritual restores connection between
physicality and gratitude — vitality as sacred
expression.)

_____

_____

JOURNAL REFLECTION

How does my body express joy and strength?
What activities make me feel alive and empowered?
How can I celebrate my body daily?

_____

_____

MEAL & MOVEMENT

Eat fresh, energizing foods — smoothies, whole grains,
hydration. Move with playfulness — dance, jog, or stretch
to awaken vitality.

Today I nourish my body with:

_____

Today I move with intention through:

_____

"I honor my body's rhythm and radiance."

EVENING GRATITUDE

Feeling strong helped me feel:

_____

_____

DAY 171-Joyful Embodiment & Radiance — Living from Love, Pleasure, and Vitality

"Authentic expression is my art form."

MORNING RITUAL

Take a breath and whisper: "It's safe to be fully me."
Wear something today that makes you feel alive — color, jewelry, scent, or even a song that matches your energy.
(This ritual reclaims authentic expression as an act of joy and confidence.)

MEAL & MOVEMENT

Eat intuitively — let your senses guide you. Move creatively — dance, paint, or walk while humming your favorite tune.

Today I nourish my body with:

Today I move with intention through:

JOURNAL REFLECTION

How do I express myself creatively or emotionally?
Where do I still hide or hold back?
What does freedom of expression look like for me?

"Expression is liberation."

EVENING GRATITUDE

Authenticity helped me feel:

DAY 172-Joyful Embodiment & Radiance — Living from Love, Pleasure, and Vitality

"Playfulness keeps my spirit light and creative."

MORNING RITUAL

Before starting your responsibilities, pause and whisper:
"Today, I make space for play."
Think of one small fun thing you can do today — something that makes you laugh or feel free.
(This ritual reconnects participants with their inner child — the source of spontaneity and flow.)

MEAL & MOVEMENT

Eat light, energizing meals that feel fun — maybe breakfast for dinner or a new flavor. Move playfully — dance, jump, skip, or stretch with humor and joy.

Today I nourish my body with:

Today I move with intention through:

JOURNAL REFLECTION

When was the last time I truly played?
How does play heal or recharge me?
How can I bring lightheartedness to my routine?

"Play is presence in joy."

EVENING GRATITUDE
Laughter helped me feel:

DAY 173-Joyful Embodiment & Radiance — Living from Love, Pleasure, and Vitality

"My light is meant to be seen."

MORNING RITUAL

Stand tall, close your eyes, and imagine light shining from your heart, filling the room.
Whisper: "I give myself permission to shine."
(This ritual removes fear of visibility — shining as a service, not performance.)

MEAL & MOVEMENT

Eat meals that make you feel vibrant — bright fruits, energizing grains. Move expansively — arms open, chest lifted, confident stance.

Today I nourish my body with:

Today I move with intention through:

JOURNAL REFLECTION

What dimmed my light in the past?
What helps me feel radiant now?
How can I share my light without fear?

"I am a vessel of light and joy."

EVENING GRATITUDE

Laughter helped me feel:

DAY 174-Joyful Embodiment & Radiance — Living from Love, Pleasure, and Vitality

"Each breath is a reason to celebrate."

MORNING RITUAL

Take a deep breath and smile. Whisper: "Today, I celebrate being alive."
Light a candle or play a song that feels like a personal anthem. Move, sing, or simply savor the beauty of existing.
(This ritual closes the week by transforming daily life into a celebration — joy as devotion.)

_____

_____

JOURNAL REFLECTION

What am I celebrating about my life today?
How has joy changed the way I experience growth?
How can I carry this energy into tomorrow?

_____

_____

MEAL & MOVEMENT

Eat with gratitude — something that delights the senses. Move joyfully — dance, stretch, walk, or sway to music you love.

Today I nourish my body with:

_____

Today I move with intention through:

_____

"My life is the celebration."

EVENING GRATITUDE

Living with gratitude helped me feel:

_____

_____

DAY 175-Connection & Authentic Relationships — Embodying Love in Action

"True connection begins with being fully here."

MORNING RITUAL

As you interact with others today, practice full attention.
Put away distractions, look into their eyes, and listen deeply. Before speaking, whisper silently:
"May this moment be sacred connection."
(This ritual transforms ordinary moments into conscious exchanges of energy.)

JOURNAL REFLECTION

How do I show up when I'm truly present with others?
Who in my life deserves my full attention today?
How does presence strengthen my relationships?

MEAL & MOVEMENT

Eat meals with loved ones if possible — without devices. Move socially — a walk, yoga class, or shared activity that fosters presence.

Today I nourish my body with:

Today I move with intention through:

"Presence deepens love."

EVENING GRATITUDE

Presence helped me feel:

TRUEJOY-LIVING

A YEAR OF TRANSFORMATION

DAY 176-Connection & Authentic Relationships — Embodying Love in Action

"My words build bridges, not walls."

MORNING RITUAL

Before speaking today, take a breath and whisper:
"May my words come from kindness."
If a conversation feels tense, pause — breathe through the heart before replying.
(This ritual teaches emotional regulation in connection — empathy expressed through communication.)

MEAL & MOVEMENT

Eat soothing foods that calm the nervous system — soups, teas. Move gently — yoga or stretching that opens the chest and throat.

Today I nourish my body with:

Today I move with intention through:

JOURNAL REFLECTION

How does compassion change the way I communicate?
When do I find it hardest to stay kind?
What helps me speak from love instead of reaction?

"Kindness is my language."

EVENING GRATITUDE

Heart-centered words helped me feel:

DAY 177-Connection & Authentic Relationships — Embodying Love in Action

"Listening is love in action."

MORNING RITUAL

Set an intention before your first conversation:
"Today, I listen with an open heart."
Pause before responding — let silence hold space.
Feel the energy shift when someone feels truly heard.
(This ritual elevates listening from habit to healing — presence as the purest gift.)

_____

_____

JOURNAL REFLECTION

When do I feel most heard and understood?
How can I offer that gift to others?
What wisdom arises when I truly listen?

_____

_____

MEAL & MOVEMENT

Eat simple, grounding meals — chewing slowly in silence to practice mindful listening. Move with awareness — walking meditation or breathwork to tune inward.

Today I nourish my body with:

_____

Today I move with intention through:

_____

"Listening opens hearts."

EVENING GRATITUDE

Understanding helped me feel:

_____

_____

DAY 178-Connection & Authentic Relationships — Embodying Love in Action

"Love is freedom, not possession."

MORNING RITUAL

Place a hand over your heart and whisper:
"I release expectations. I choose love without control."
Visualize every relationship surrounded by soft light — no cords, only flow.
(This ritual balances love with freedom — teaching non-attachment as sacred respect.)

MEAL & MOVEMENT

Eat light, expansive meals — fruits, greens, herbal infusions. Move freely — flowing yoga or dance to release energetic cords.

Today I nourish my body with:

_____

Today I move with intention through:

_____

JOURNAL REFLECTION

Where might I confuse attachment with love?
What does freedom look like in healthy connection?
How can I hold space without holding on?

_____

"I love with openness and grace."

EVENING GRATITUDE

A moment I loved without control today:

_____

TRUEJOY-LIVING

A YEAR OF TRANSFORMATION

DAY 179-Connection & Authentic Relationships — Embodying Love in Action

"As I evolve, my connections evolve with me."

MORNING RITUAL

Close your eyes and whisper: "I attract relationships that align with my highest self."

Visualize your current circle surrounded by light — thank those who support your growth, and release any connections that no longer resonate.

(This ritual honors the evolving nature of relationships — gratitude and release as sacred balance.)

JOURNAL REFLECTION

What kind of energy do I attract in relationships now?

Who supports my evolution — and who drains it?

How can I be the kind of person I want to attract?

MEAL & MOVEMENT

Eat nurturing meals — comfort with clarity (soups, whole grains). Move reflectively — walk outdoors while reflecting on the energy you attract.

Today I nourish my body with:

_____

Today I move with intention through:

_____

"I attract love that mirrors my wholeness."

EVENING GRATITUDE

Aligned relationships helped me feel:

_____

_____

DAY 180-Connection & Authentic Relationships — Embodying Love in Action

"Forgiveness frees me."

MORNING RITUAL

Take a deep breath and whisper: "I release what no longer serves love."

Visualize someone or something from the past surrounded in light. Breathe deeply, and on the exhale, imagine letting it dissolve with peace.

(This ritual closes emotional loops — forgiveness as liberation.)

MEAL & MOVEMENT

Eat light, cleansing meals — lemon water, fruits, greens. Move gently — stretches or breathwork to release tension and grief.

Today I nourish my body with:

_____

Today I move with intention through:

_____

"I forgive to set myself free."

JOURNAL REFLECTION

Who or what am I ready to forgive?

What emotions am I holding onto that weigh me down?

How will forgiveness create space for peace?

_____

EVENING GRATITUDE

Forgiving helped me feel:

_____

_____

DAY 181–Connection & Authentic Relationships — Embodying Love in Action

"Love flows to me, through me, and around me."

MORNING RITUAL

Take three deep breaths and whisper:
"I am open to give and receive love freely."
Visualize a circle of light — friends, family, community —
all connected through shared compassion and support.
(This ritual integrates love as a collective energy field —
community as reflection of inner harmony.)

JOURNAL REFLECTION

How does love show up in my life right now?
Who reminds me that I'm supported and valued?
How can I express gratitude for the love that surrounds
me?

MEAL & MOVEMENT

Eat community-style meals — cook or share with loved
ones. Move with connection — group walk, shared
yoga, or joyful dance.

Today I nourish my body with:

_____

Today I move with intention through:

_____

"I am one with love itself."

EVENING GRATITUDE

Someone who showed me love today:

_____

_____

DAY 182-Living in Flow — Trust, Synchronicity, and Divine Timing

"Everything unfolds in perfect timing."

MORNING RITUAL

Take a deep breath and whisper: "I release the need to control."

Visualize your energy as a river — steady, effortless, guided by an unseen current. Let go of the need to push. Simply float, trusting the flow.

(This ritual begins the shift from control to trust — the core of embodied flow.)

JOURNAL REFLECTION

Where am I trying too hard to control the outcome?
What would trusting the flow look like instead?
How does surrender feel in my body?

MEAL & MOVEMENT

Eat soft, soothing foods — soups, teas, warm grains. Move fluidly — flowing yoga, tai chi, or slow stretching.

Today I nourish my body with:

_____

Today I move with intention through:

_____

"I trust the river of life to carry me."

EVENING GRATITUDE

Surrendering helped me feel:

_____

_____

DAY 183-Living in Flow — Trust, Synchronicity, and Divine Timing

"The right things unfold at the right time."

MORNING RITUAL

As you begin your day, whisper: "There is no rush — I am exactly where I need to be."
Pause before major actions and sense the timing — if it feels tight or forced, wait. If it feels light and natural, move.
(This ritual deepens intuitive flow — action guided by resonance, not urgency.)

JOURNAL REFLECTION

What happens when I rush versus when I flow?
How does divine timing show up in my life?
What am I learning to trust will come when ready?

MEAL & MOVEMENT

Eat at natural times — honor hunger cues. Move rhythmically — walking, dancing, or cycling to match your energy flow.

Today I nourish my body with:

Today I move with intention through:

"I move in harmony with time."

EVENING GRATITUDE

Something that aligned effortlessly today:

DAY 184-Living in Flow — Trust, Synchronicity, and Divine Timing

"I follow life's guidance with open hands."

MORNING RITUAL

Close your eyes and whisper:
"Show me where to go today, life."
Move through your day with curiosity instead of planning — follow subtle nudges, coincidences, or invitations.
(This ritual trains receptivity — becoming a conscious co-creator rather than a controller.)

MEAL & MOVEMENT

Eat intuitively — what your body calls for. Move freely — walk without direction, dance without choreography.

Today I nourish my body with:

_____

Today I move with intention through:

_____

JOURNAL REFLECTION

How does life communicate with me?
When was I last surprised by grace or synchronicity?
What guidance did I receive today?

_____

_____

"I am guided with ease and clarity."

EVENING GRATITUDE

Following flow helped me feel:

_____

_____

DAY 185-Living in Flow — Trust, Synchronicity, and Divine Timing

"I am aligned with the magic of the universe."

MORNING RITUAL

Whisper: "Today I stay open to signs and synchronicities."
Throughout the day, notice repeated numbers, songs, words, or encounters that seem meaningful — record them later.
(This ritual cultivates awareness of universal dialogue — connection beyond logic.)

MEAL & MOVEMENT

Eat foods that heighten intuition — clean water, greens, berries. Move with openness — heart-opening poses, gentle breath-work.

Today I nourish my body with:

_____

Today I move with intention through:

_____

JOURNAL REFLECTION

What synchronicities appeared today?
What could they be guiding me toward?
How does noticing them make me feel connected?

_____

"I walk hand-in-hand with divine alignment."

EVENING GRATITUDE

One synchronicity I experienced today:

_____

_____

DAY 186-Living in Flow — Trust, Synchronicity, and Divine Timing

"Uncertainty is the space where miracles grow."

MORNING RITUAL

Take a deep breath and whisper: "I relax into the mystery."
As you move through the day, release the need for answers
— instead, notice what unfolds when you trust.
(This ritual builds comfort in uncertainty — the essence of
spiritual maturity.)

MEAL & MOVEMENT

Eat nourishing, grounding meals — roots, lentils,
soups. Move gently — meditative walk, slow yoga.

Today I nourish my body with:

Today I move with intention through:

JOURNAL REFLECTION

How do I react to not knowing?
What could the unknown be teaching me?
Where can I practice more faith than fear?

"The unknown is fertile ground for miracles."

EVENING GRATITUDE

Trusting uncertainty helped me feel:

DAY 187-Living in Flow — Trust, Synchronicity, and Divine Timing

"I create through ease, not effort."

MORNING RITUAL

Whisper: "I allow things to unfold without resistance."

As you move through tasks, check in: Am I pushing, or am I allowing?

Shift from tension to trust whenever you feel strain.

(This ritual releases attachment to results — replacing willpower with flow power.)

MEAL & MOVEMENT

Eat light and nourishing foods — steamed veggies, soups, water. Move softly — yin yoga or stretching to release tightness.

Today I nourish my body with:

_____

Today I move with intention through:

_____

JOURNAL REFLECTION

Where am I still forcing outcomes?

How can I invite more allowing into those areas?

What changes when I soften into flow?

_____

"I allow life to be easy."

EVENING GRATITUDE

Letting go helped me feel:

_____

_____

DAY 188-Living in Flow — Trust, Synchronicity, and Divine Timing

"I dance with life in perfect harmony."

MORNING RITUAL

Take a deep breath and imagine your heart beating in rhythm with the earth's pulse.

Whisper: "I am in sync with life's divine rhythm."

Let music or movement guide you — sway, breathe, or simply notice life's cadence in everything around you.

(This ritual completes the flow cycle — unity between self and existence.)

MEAL & MOVEMENT

Eat balanced, nourishing meals — honoring both energy and rest. Move rhythmically — dance, flow yoga, or breath-to-movement.

Today I nourish my body with:

_____

Today I move with intention through:

_____

JOURNAL REFLECTION

What does living in rhythm feel like to me?

Where am I still out of sync?

How can I bring more harmony into daily life?

_____

"I am one with the pulse of the universe.

EVENING GRATITUDE

Harmony helped me feel:

_____

_____

DAY 189-Integration & Reflection— Living as the Whole Self

"I honor my evolution with gratitude."

MORNING RITUAL

Take a slow, deep breath and whisper: "Thank you, Self, for showing up."

Look back over your journey — the moments of growth, the courage, the resilience.

(This ritual roots integration through gratitude — reflection as nourishment.)

JOURNAL REFLECTION

How have I changed since the beginning of this journey?

What lessons will I carry forward daily?

How does it feel to honor myself for simply staying the course?

MEAL & MOVEMENT

Eat grounding meals — soups, grains, tea. Move softly — stretching or walking while reflecting on your growth.

Today I nourish my body with:

Today I move with intention through:

"I am grateful for who I've become."

EVENING GRATITUDE

Reflecting helped me feel:

DAY 190-Integration & Reflection—
Living as the Whole Self

"Every part of me belongs."

MORNING RITUAL

Close your eyes and whisper: "I welcome every
part of me — past, present, becoming."
Visualize all versions of yourself — the child, the
dreamer, the achiever, the healer — gathering in
one warm, loving embrace.
(This ritual unites fragmented aspects —
integration through compassion.)

_____

_____

JOURNAL REFLECTION

What parts of myself have I rejected or ignored?
How can I welcome them home with love?
What does wholeness feel like to me?

_____

_____

MEAL & MOVEMENT

Eat balanced, whole meals — sweet and savory,
warm and cool. Move holistically — combine flow
and stillness (yoga, walking, or intuitive movement).

Today I nourish my body with:

_____

Today I move with intention through:

_____

"I am complete and united."

EVENING GRATITUDE

Integration helped me feel:

_____

_____

DAY 191—Integration & Reflection—
Living as the Whole Self
"Both my light and my shadow make me whole."

MORNING RITUAL

Take a deep breath and whisper: "I meet myself with honesty and love."

Think of one aspect of yourself you've judged — send it compassion. It has always been trying to protect or guide you in some way.

(This ritual restores balance — wholeness includes acceptance of contrast.)

MEAL & MOVEMENT

Eat grounding foods — root vegetables, dark greens. Move in balance — alternating stillness and motion to mirror inner duality.

Today I nourish my body with:

_____

Today I move with intention through:

_____

JOURNAL REFLECTION

What "shadow" aspects of me are ready to be understood? What gifts might they hold?

How does accepting all of me change my energy?

_____

"Light and shadow dance in harmony within me."

EVENING GRATITUDE

Acceptance helped me feel:

_____

_____

DAY 192—Integration & Reflection— Living as the Whole Self

"Peace is my natural rhythm."

MORNING RITUAL

Sit in stillness and whisper: "I align with the rhythm of peace."

Breathe into your heart and imagine balance flowing through every cell — a quiet, steady pulse of harmony.

(This ritual integrates emotional, mental, and physical equilibrium — inner unity made tangible.)

MEAL & MOVEMENT

Eat light but steady meals — balanced nutrients, hydration. Move smoothly — yoga or tai chi focused on breath alignment.

Today I nourish my body with:

_____

Today I move with intention through:

_____

JOURNAL REFLECTION

What does inner harmony feel like in my body?
Where do I feel imbalance, and how can I soothe it?
How does harmony change the way I respond to life?

_____

"Peace lives within me always."

EVENING GRATITUDE

Harmony helped me feel:

_____

_____

DAY 193-Integration & Reflection—
Living as the Whole Self
"I am the embodiment of my potential."

MORNING RITUAL

Whisper: "I choose to show up as my highest self today."
Visualize yourself radiating confidence, calm, and love.
Let every decision today flow from that energy.
(This ritual reinforces identity embodiment — being rather than becoming.)

_____

_____

JOURNAL REFLECTION

How does my highest self think, speak, and act?
What can I do today to live from that version of me?
What environments help that energy flourish?

_____

_____

MEAL & MOVEMENT

Eat nourishing, elevated meals — colorful, vibrant foods. Move with posture — standing tall, open-hearted, centered.

Today I nourish my body with:

_____

Today I move with intention through:

_____

"My higher self and I are one."

EVENING GRATITUDE

A moment I embodied my highest self today:

_____

_____

DAY 194-Integration & Reflection— Living as the Whole Self

"Every moment is an opportunity to live with intention."

MORNING RITUAL

Light a candle or simply breathe in gratitude.
Whisper: "This day is sacred."
Move slowly through your morning — each action
(drinking, walking, speaking) as if it were a prayer.
(This ritual transforms the ordinary into the divine
— sacred living through mindfulness.)

_____

_____

JOURNAL REFLECTION

What makes a moment sacred to me?
How can I bring reverence to my routine?
How does seeing life as ceremony change my
energy?

_____

_____

MEAL & MOVEMENT

Eat mindfully — savor textures, colors, smells. Move
reverently — gentle flow or meditative walking.

Today I nourish my body with:

_____

Today I move with intention through:

_____

"Life itself is my practice."

EVENING GRATITUDE

Living intentionally helped me feel:

_____

_____

DAY 195–Integration & Reflection— Living as the Whole Self

"I have arrived — peace lives within me."

MORNING RITUAL

Take a slow, deep breath and whisper: "I am home in myself."

Feel your body, your breath, your awareness — everything returning to center. Now, you simply be.

(This ritual seals the transformation — self-realization as the true destination.)

_____

_____

JOURNAL REFLECTION

What does "home within myself" feel like?

What am I most grateful for in this journey?

How will I continue living from this wholeness daily?

_____

_____

MEAL & MOVEMENT

Eat comforting, heart-centered meals — foods that feel like "home." Move gently — slow walking, soft stretching, or complete stillness.

Today I nourish my body with:

_____

Today I move with intention through:

_____

"I am home. I am whole. I am TrueJoy."

EVENING GRATITUDE

Wholeness helped me feel:

_____

_____

DAY 196-Review, Renewal & Living the Flow

"I honor every step that led me here."

MORNING RITUAL

Whisper: "Today, I celebrate me."
Light a candle or play your favorite song. Reflect on how much you've evolved — emotionally, spiritually, physically.
Celebrate without condition or comparison.
(This ritual cultivates self-recognition — joy in the act of completion.)

MEAL & MOVEMENT

Eat something that feels like celebration — vibrant, colorful, nourishing. Move joyfully — dance, walk, or stretch to music that lights you up.

Today I nourish my body with:

_____

Today I move with intention through:

_____

JOURNAL REFLECTION

What am I most proud of this year?
What moments shaped my strength the most?
How can I celebrate progress, not just results?

_____

"I am worthy of celebration."

EVENING GRATITUDE

Self-recognition helped me feel:

_____

DAY 197–Review, Renewal & Living the Flow

"I thank the past and set it free."

MORNING RITUAL

Take three deep breaths and whisper: "Thank you for everything, even what I didn't understand."
Write a short letter to the past year — acknowledging challenges and blessings — then tear, burn, or safely discard it with gratitude.
(This ritual clears energetic space for renewal.)

MEAL & MOVEMENT

Eat light and cleansing — soups, greens, herbal tea. Move gently — restorative yoga, stretching, or a releasing walk.

Today I nourish my body with:

_____

Today I move with intention through:

_____

JOURNAL REFLECTION

What am I ready to let go of?
What am I grateful to leave behind with love?

_____

_____

"Releasing makes space for renewal."

EVENING GRATITUDE

Something I released with thanks today:

_____

_____

DAY 198–Review, Renewal & Living the Flow
"I welcome new beginnings with open arms."

MORNING RITUAL

Whisper: "I am ready for renewal."
Visualize golden light washing through your body —
refreshing, recharging, and awakening your next-level
vision. Imagine this light carrying inspiration into the year
ahead.
(This ritual reactivates creative energy for the next cycle.)

JOURNAL REFLECTION

What feels ready to be reborn within me?
What dreams or callings are beginning to stir?
How can I nurture this fresh energy gently?

MEAL & MOVEMENT

Eat revitalizing meals — fruits, greens, lemon water. Move
dynamically — walks, gentle cardio, or energy-focused
stretching.

Today I nourish my body with:

Today I move with intention through:

"I welcome what's next with joy."

EVENING GRATITUDE
Feeling refreshed helped me feel:

TRUEJOY-LIVING
A YEAR OF TRANSFORMATION

DAY 199–Review, Renewal & Living the Flow

"Clearing creates clarity."

MORNING RITUAL

Whisper: "I make space for new blessings."
Declutter one small area — your desk, closet, or
digital space. Notice how lightness follows letting
go.
(This ritual grounds renewal in physical action —
embodiment through space.)

JOURNAL REFLECTION

What am I ready to clear from my environment or
energy?
How does physical space mirror my internal world?
How can I maintain sacred space moving forward?

MEAL & MOVEMENT

Eat light and minimal — nourish clarity. Move
intentionally — organize, clean, or gentle
stretching while breathing deeply.

Today I nourish my body with:

Today I move with intention through:

"The clearer I am, the freer I feel."

EVENING GRATITUDE

Making space helped me feel:

TRUEJOY-LIVING

A YEAR OF TRANSFORMATION

DAY 200-Review, Renewal & Living the Flow

"Purpose is my guiding light."

MORNING RITUAL

Place your hands over your heart and whisper: "I remember why I began."
Reflect on the moment that brought you to this path — your first spark of transformation.
Reconnect with that essence, now matured through experience.
(This ritual rekindles meaning — the foundation of sustainable purpose.)

JOURNAL REFLECTION

What was my "why" when I began this journey?
Has it evolved or deepened?
What keeps me devoted to my growth?

MEAL & MOVEMENT

Eat warm, comforting meals that ground intention. Move slowly — stretching or yoga with focus on the heart and breath.

Today I nourish my body with:

Today I move with intention through:

"Purpose anchors my path."

EVENING GRATITUDE

Remembering my why helped me feel:

TRUEJOY-LIVING

A YEAR OF TRANSFORMATION

DAY 201-Review, Renewal & Living the Flow

"I am the conscious author of my next story."

MORNING RITUAL

Whisper: "What am I ready to create next?"
Spend time envisioning the next season of your life
— not through pressure, but possibility.
Write or draw your dreams without limits.
(This ritual reclaims creative authorship —
conscious co-creation.)

MEAL & MOVEMENT

Eat inspiring foods — bright colors, spices, flavors
that feel new. Move expansively — walks, yoga, or
music that stirs imagination.

Today I nourish my body with:

_____

Today I move with intention through:

_____

JOURNAL REFLECTION

What themes will define my next chapter?
What does living in alignment look like from here?
What habits or rituals support my new vision?

_____

_____

"I create my reality with joy."

EVENING GRATITUDE

A new possibility that inspired me today:

_____

_____

TRUEJOY-LIVING

A YEAR OF TRANSFORMATION

DAY 202–Review, Renewal & Living the Flow

"I walk forward with faith, grace, and gratitude."

MORNING RITUAL

Take a deep breath and whisper: "I trust what's next."

Walk outside or near a window.

Look toward the horizon and imagine life guiding you gently toward your next unfolding.

(This ritual merges surrender and excitement — trust in continuous transformation.)

JOURNAL REFLECTION

What am I most grateful for as I step forward?

What do I trust about myself now that I didn't before?

How will I keep walking in faith?

MEAL & MOVEMENT

Eat harmonizing foods — light yet grounding.
Move rhythmically — walk or flow with gentle forward motion.

Today I nourish my body with:

_____

Today I move with intention through:

_____

"I trust myself. I trust life."

EVENING GRATITUDE

Faith helped me feel:

_____

_____

DAY 203-Integration Ceremony, Renewal Rituals& Living the Flow

"I celebrate endings as sacred beginnings."

MORNING RITUAL

Light a candle or simply breathe in gratitude.
Whisper: "This chapter is complete, and I honor what it taught me."
Visualize the past year as a glowing circle — each phase shining as part of a larger whole.
(This ritual helps participants integrate completion with peace — not finality, but wholeness.)

_____

_____

JOURNAL REFLECTION

What cycles in my life are closing now?

What have I learned from their completion?

How do endings prepare space for new beginnings?

_____

_____

MEAL & MOVEMENT

Eat comforting, nourishing meals — foods that feel like home. Move in gentle circles — swaying, slow yoga, or walking loops to honor cycles.

Today I nourish my body with:

_____

Today I move with intention through:

_____

"I honor what has been and welcome what's next."

EVENING GRATITUDE

Completion helped me feel:

_____

_____

DAY 204-Integration Ceremony, Renewal Rituals& Living the Flow

"I celebrate endings as sacred beginnings."

MORNING RITUAL

Set aside sacred space — a candle, journal, music, or nature. Whisper: "I honor myself through ritual."

Choose one element to symbolize renewal — water (cleansing), air (breath), earth (stability), or fire (transformation). Spend time journaling or meditating with that element.

JOURNAL REFLECTION

Which element reflects where I am in my journey?

How can I honor renewal through ritual more often?

What am I symbolically birthing today?

MEAL & MOVEMENT

Eat foods tied to your chosen element — grounding roots (earth), fresh fruits (water), light greens (air), or spicy meals (fire). Move with intention — mirror the energy of your element.

Today I nourish my body with:

Today I move with intention through:

"Ritual makes my growth sacred."

EVENING GRATITUDE

Ceremony helped me feel:

DAY 205-Integration Ceremony, Renewal Rituals& Living the Flow

"I walk the path of alignment with devotion."

MORNING RITUAL

Place a hand on your heart and whisper: "I recommit to my truth." Visualize the six pillars — Ground, Awaken, Manifest, Evolve, Conquer, Embody — forming a glowing lotus within your chest. Each petal shines with balance, symbolizing your integrated journey.
(This ritual renews devotion — the daily return to what matters most.)

JOURNAL REFLECTION

What practices keep me in alignment?
How can I sustain balance in my everyday rhythm?
Which pillar will I revisit first when I need recalibration?

MEAL & MOVEMENT

Eat foods from all color groups — diversity mirrors wholeness. Move holistically — a full-body flow or mindful walk connecting breath and intention.

Today I nourish my body with:

_____

Today I move with intention through:

_____

"I am in continuous alignment with my truth."

EVENING GRATITUDE

Recommitting helped me feel:

_____

_____

DAY 206-Integration Ceremony, Renewal Rituals& Living the Flow

"Growth is my natural rhythm."

MORNING RITUAL

Take three slow breaths. Whisper: "I evolve with grace, not effort."

Visualize yourself years from now — peaceful, radiant, continually learning and softening into wisdom.

(This ritual celebrates transformation as ongoing — an infinite spiral, not a straight line.)

_____

_____

JOURNAL REFLECTION

What does lifelong transformation mean to me now?

How do I stay open to evolving without chasing change?

What lessons will always guide me forward?

_____

_____

MEAL & MOVEMENT

Eat colorful, nourishing meals — variety symbolizes change embraced. Move intuitively — flow between energy and rest as the body desires.

Today I nourish my body with:

_____

Today I move with intention through:

_____

"I evolve forever in peace."

EVENING GRATITUDE

Embracing lifelong growth helped me feel:

_____

_____

DAY 207-Integration Ceremony, Renewal Rituals& Living the Flow

"Every season has purpose."

MORNING RITUAL

Whisper: "I honor the season I'm in."

Notice nature — the temperature, colors, light.

Ask, "What is this season teaching me?"

Reflect on how your own rhythm mirrors nature's ebb and flow.

(This ritual strengthens seasonal awareness — embodiment beyond self.)

JOURNAL REFLECTION

What season of growth am I in right now?

How does nature's rhythm mirror my inner rhythm?

How can I live more in tune with natural cycles?

MEAL & MOVEMENT

Eat seasonally — foods grown locally or fresh in your area. Move in alignment with the climate — grounding in winter, flowing in spring, energizing in summer, restorative in fall.

Today I nourish my body with:

Today I move with intention through:

"I move with the rhythm of life."

EVENING GRATITUDE

Something the current season taught me today:

DAY 208-Integration Ceremony, Renewal Rituals& Living the Flow

"My life is my message."

MORNING RITUAL

Whisper: "I embody what I wish to see in the world."
Today, let your energy inspire others — through kindness, laughter, authenticity, or quiet strength.
You are the living example of alignment.
(This ritual integrates purpose through presence — leadership through embodiment.)

JOURNAL REFLECTION

How does my daily life reflect my growth?
What does it mean to "live my message"?
How do I inspire others simply by being myself?

MEAL & MOVEMENT

Eat vibrant, life-affirming meals — community foods or shared dishes. Move in joy — walk, dance, or connect socially.

Today I nourish my body with:

_____

Today I move with intention through:

_____

"I live my truth beautifully and boldly."

EVENING GRATITUDE

A way I embodied transformation today:

_____

DAY 209-Integration Ceremony, Renewal Rituals& Living the Flow

"Gratitude turns my transformation into grace."

MORNING RITUAL

Write down ten things — big and small — you're grateful for from this journey.

Whisper: "Thank you for this path, this peace, this purpose."

(This ritual anchors closure in appreciation — gratitude as integration.)

MEAL & MOVEMENT

Eat a favorite comfort meal mindfully. Move gently — gratitude walk, stretching, or slow dance to your favorite song.

Today I nourish my body with:

Today I move with intention through:

JOURNAL REFLECTION

Who or what supported me most on this path?

What am I most thankful for in myself?

How can I keep gratitude as a daily practice?

"Thank you, life, for everything."

EVENING GRATITUDE

The thing I'm most grateful for today:

DAY 210-Integration Ceremony, Renewal Rituals& Living the Flow

"Every ending is a beginning in disguise."

MORNING RITUAL

Take a deep breath and whisper: "I begin again, with trust and joy."

Stand in front of a mirror or step outside — smile softly.

You've come full circle.

(This final ritual initiates renewal — transformation as continuous flow.)

_____

_____

JOURNAL REFLECTION

How will I live TrueJoy beyond this year?

What practices will I carry forward daily?

What am I most excited to create next?

_____

_____

MEAL & MOVEMENT

Eat intuitively — whatever feels most nourishing. Move with freedom — dance, stretch, or simply breathe in gratitude for life.

Today I nourish my body with:

_____

Today I move with intention through:

_____

"I am the flow. I am the joy. I am the transformation."

EVENING GRATITUDE

Beginning again helped me feel:

_____

_____

DAY 211-Living the Flow
Everyday Practice
"Presence is my daily practice."

MORNING RITUAL
Before rising, place your hand on your heart.
Whisper: "I awaken in awareness."
Notice your breath, your body, the quiet before movement.
(Presence becomes the anchor that starts every flow-filled day.)

JOURNAL REFLECTION
What helps me feel most present in the morning?
How can I pause before reacting today?
What anchors me when I drift from awareness?

MEAL & MOVEMENT
Eat a nourishing breakfast that grounds you — oatmeal, tea, or fruit. Move gently — stretch or walk while noticing each step.

Today I nourish my body with:

_____

Today I move with intention through:

_____

"I am here — now."

EVENING GRATITUDE
Awareness helped me feel:

_____

_____

DAY 212-Living the Flow
Everyday Practice
"Action and stillness dance in harmony."

MORNING RITUAL

Write your top three priorities. Then sit in silence for two minutes before beginning them.

(This harmonizes productivity with peace.)

JOURNAL REFLECTION

Where do I over-do or under-rest?
What would balance feel like today?
How does rest amplify my results?

MEAL & MOVEMENT

Eat steady-energy meals — grains, greens, water. Move consciously — alternate effort and rest.

Today I nourish my body with:

Today I move with intention through:

"Balance is my power."

EVENING GRATITUDE

One balanced moment today:

TRUEJOY-LIVING

A YEAR OF TRANSFORMATION

DAY 213–Living the Flow
Everyday Practice
"Roots first, then rise."

MORNING RITUAL
Stand barefoot (or visualize roots from your feet). Breathe down into the earth.
Whisper: "I am supported."

MEAL & MOVEMENT
Eat warm, earthy meals — soups, root veggies.
Move with strength — yoga poses that root you (mountain, warrior).

Today I nourish my body with:

_____

Today I move with intention through:

_____

JOURNAL REFLECTION
What grounds me emotionally?
How does stability help me expand?
Where can I root deeper before reaching higher?

"Grounded, I grow with grace."

EVENING GRATITUDE
A grounding action I took today:

_____

_____

DAY 214–Living the Flow
Everyday Practice
"Gratitude multiplies my joy."

MORNING RITUAL

List three things you're grateful for before checking your phone.
(Sets the vibration of abundance early.)

MEAL & MOVEMENT

Eat colorful meals that uplift mood. Move joyfully — walk or stretch while silently saying thank you.

Today I nourish my body with:

_____

Today I move with intention through:

_____

JOURNAL REFLECTION

What am I thankful for right now?
How does gratitude shift my energy?
Who can I thank today?

"Thank you for this beautiful day."

EVENING GRATITUDE

A gratitude moment I experienced:

_____

DAY 215-Living the Flow
Everyday Practice
"My inner voice always leads me home."

MORNING RITUAL

Sit in stillness and ask: "What do I need to know today?"
Write the first whisper that arises — trust it.

MEAL & MOVEMENT

Eat intuitively — choose what your body asks for. Move freely — flow or dance to match your mood.

Today I nourish my body with:

Today I move with intention through:

JOURNAL REFLECTION

How did intuition speak to me today?
What happens when I trust it?
Where am I learning to listen deeper?

"I trust my inner wisdom"

EVENING GRATITUDE

A moment I followed intuition:

DAY 216-Living the Flow
Everyday Practice
"My energy is sacred fuel."

MORNING RITUAL

Check your inner battery. Whisper:
"What do I need to feel vibrant today?"
Honor the answer — rest,
movement, sunlight, water.

MEAL & MOVEMENT

Eat high-vibration meals — fruits, greens, protein.
Move to energize — brisk walk, power yoga,
breathwork.

Today I nourish my body with:

_____

Today I move with intention through:

_____

JOURNAL REFLECTION

What drains or recharges my energy most?
How did I nourish my vitality today?
What boundaries protect my peace?

"I honor my vitality."

EVENING GRATITUDE
A way I cared for my energy today:

_____

_____

DAY 217–Living the Flow
Everyday Practice
"Patience keeps me in peace."

MORNING RITUAL

Whisper: "I move at the pace of grace."
Whenever impatience arises today,
take one mindful breath before
acting.

_____

_____

JOURNAL REFLECTION

Where do I rush or force outcomes?
What happens when I slow down?
How can I make patience a strength?

_____

_____

MEAL & MOVEMENT

Eat slowly, savoring flavors. Move gently — tai
chi, slow walk, or restorative stretching.

Today I nourish my body with:

_____

Today I move with intention through:

_____

"I am peace in motion."

EVENING GRATITUDE

A moment I chose patience today:

_____

_____

DAY 218–Living the Flow
Everyday Practice
"Each breath returns me to balance."

MORNING RITUAL

Before you rise, take 5 slow breaths. Whisper: "I follow my breath back home."
Throughout the day, pause often to breathe consciously—between emails, conversations, and meals.
(This ritual trains nervous-system awareness; breath becomes your compass.)

_____

_____

JOURNAL REFLECTION

When do I forget to breathe fully?
How does conscious breathing shift my mood or pace?
What practices remind me to pause?

_____

_____

MEAL & MOVEMENT

Eat lightly — greens, water, fruit. Move with breath awareness — inhale to lengthen, exhale to soften.

Today I nourish my body with:

_____

Today I move with intention through:

_____

"Breath carries my peace."

EVENING GRATITUDE

A moment breath grounded me today:

_____

_____

DAY 219–Living the Flow
Everyday Practice
"Less effort, more essence."

MORNING RITUAL

Look around your space and whisper:
"Today I choose simple."
Clear one small area or simplify one task
—creating physical ease that mirrors
inner ease.
(Simplicity reveals space for joy.)

MEAL & MOVEMENT

Eat clean, minimal ingredients. Move gently—
stretch or stroll without agenda.

Today I nourish my body with:

_____

Today I move with intention through:

_____

JOURNAL REFLECTION

Where am I overcomplicating things?
How can simplicity bring relief?
What one thing can I release today?

"Simplicity is serenity."

EVENING GRATITUDE

A simple joy I experienced:

_____

_____

DAY 220-Living the Flow
Everyday Practice
"Curiosity keeps my heart open."

MORNING RITUAL

Whisper: "I meet today with wonder."
Notice something ordinary as if for the first time—
the texture of sunlight, the taste of water.
(Curiosity transforms monotony into mindfulness.)

MEAL & MOVEMENT

Eat something new or prepared differently. Move
playfully—try a new route, rhythm, or song.

Today I nourish my body with:

_____

Today I move with intention through:

_____

JOURNAL REFLECTION

What new insight or experience surprised me today?
How does curiosity change the way I listen or learn?
Where can I replace judgment with wonder?

"I stay open to discovery."

EVENING GRATITUDE

A moment curiosity expanded me:

_____

DAY 221–Living the Flow
Everyday Practice
"Kindness is my compass."

MORNING RITUAL

Whisper: "I am enough, and so is everyone else."
Send silent blessings to three people who come to mind.
(Kindness dissolves competition; compassion breeds calm.)

MEAL & MOVEMENT

Eat foods that comfort gently—soups, teas. Move softly—heart-opening stretches or slow yoga.

Today I nourish my body with:

Today I move with intention through:

JOURNAL REFLECTION

Where did comparison appear today?
How can I turn it into inspiration?
How does kindness shift my energy toward others?

"Kindness connects me to joy."

EVENING GRATITUDE

A kind act I offered today:

DAY 222-Living the Flow
Everyday Practice
"Movement is meditation in motion."

MORNING RITUAL

Before moving, whisper: "I move with awareness."
Notice how your body feels—tightness, energy, rhythm—and let movement flow intuitively.
(Embodiment deepens when movement becomes mindful.)

JOURNAL REFLECTION

How did my body want to move today?
What sensations or emotions surfaced?
How can I treat movement as presence, not performance?

MEAL & MOVEMENT

Eat to fuel vitality—grains, fruit, hydration. Move slowly, matching motion to breath count.

Today I nourish my body with:

Today I move with intention through:

"Movement restores my flow."

EVENING GRATITUDE

A movement moment that centered me:

DAY 223-Living the Flow
Everyday Practice

"I eat with gratitude and grace."

MORNING RITUAL

At your first meal, whisper: "This food nourishes my energy and joy."

Eat slowly, noticing texture, color, aroma, and taste.

(Mindful nourishment roots the day in appreciation.)

MEAL & MOVEMENT

Eat without screens or distraction. Move lightly afterward—short walk or gentle breathing to aid digestion.

Today I nourish my body with:

_____

Today I move with intention through:

_____

JOURNAL REFLECTION

How does slowing down change my relationship with food?

What emotions arise around nourishment?

How can eating become an act of gratitude?

_____

"Nourishment is sacred."

EVENING GRATITUDE

A meal I fully savored:

_____

_____

DAY 224–Living the Flow
Everyday Practice
"Stillness restores my soul."

MORNING RITUAL

Whisper: "I will close this day with peace."
Schedule 5–10 minutes before bed for stillness
—no screens, no noise—just breath and being.
(Closing the day intentionally trains the body
for rest and reflection.)

JOURNAL REFLECTION

What moments felt most peaceful today?
How does stillness affect my sleep and mood?
How can I protect nightly quiet time?

MEAL & MOVEMENT

Eat a light dinner—soups or teas. Move gently
before bed—stretch or breathe to unwind.

Today I nourish my body with:

Today I move with intention through:

"I rest in calm awareness."

EVENING GRATITUDE

One peaceful moment before sleep:

DAY 225-Daily Devotion & Energetic Balance

"Morning light awakens my clarity and calm."

MORNING RITUAL

Before checking your phone, step outside or near a window. Whisper: "I receive this new day with open heart."
Notice the quality of light, the temperature, the sound around you.
(Beginning with sensory presence synchronizes your rhythm with nature's.)

MEAL & MOVEMENT

Eat breakfast that feels alive — fruit, greens, water with lemon. Move slowly at first — gentle stretches to greet the day.

Today I nourish my body with:

Today I move with intention through:

JOURNAL REFLECTION

How does the morning light affect my mood?
What helps me feel awake yet peaceful?
What small ritual anchors my mornings?

"I rise in rhythm with the day."

EVENING GRATITUDE

One morning moment I cherished:

DAY 226-Daily Devotion & Energetic Balance

"I give freely and receive gracefully."

MORNING RITUAL

Whisper: "Today I will flow between offering and allowing."
Throughout the day, notice where you over-extend and where you resist help.
(Energetic balance comes from reciprocity — not sacrifice.)

_____

_____

JOURNAL REFLECTION

Where do I give too much?
How can I receive without guilt?
What does energetic equilibrium feel like?

_____

_____

MEAL & MOVEMENT

Eat balanced flavors — sweet and savory. Move in pairs — two breaths in, two breaths out; two steps forward, pause.

Today I nourish my body with:

_____

Today I move with intention through:

_____

"I am open to balance."

EVENING GRATITUDE

Something I received gratefully:

_____

_____

DAY 227-Daily Devotion & Energetic Balance

"My words create peace and power."

MORNING RITUAL

Hand on throat, breathe light into your voice.
Whisper: "I speak with clarity and
compassion."
(Truth shared from grounded energy
builds connection.)

MEAL & MOVEMENT

Drink warm tea with honey. Move with sound —
hum during stretches to release tension in the neck
and jaw.

Today I nourish my body with:

_____

Today I move with intention through:

_____

JOURNAL REFLECTION

What truth needs my voice today?
How can I speak without defense?
What happens when I listen deeply before I speak?

"My truth flows with kindness."

EVENING GRATITUDE

A moment my voice felt authentic:

_____

_____

DAY 228–Daily Devotion & Energetic Balance

"Peace is my responsibility and my gift."

MORNING RITUAL

Whisper: "I choose peace over drama."
Imagine a gentle gold light surrounding you as
an energetic boundary.
(Protection is preservation, not
separation.)

_____

JOURNAL REFLECTION

What disturbs my peace most often?
What helps me return to calm quickly?
How can I maintain boundaries lovingly?

_____

_____

MEAL & MOVEMENT

Eat soothing foods — herbal tea, soups. Move
mindfully — walk in nature to re-center.

Today I nourish my body with:

_____

Today I move with intention through:

_____

"My peace is sacred."

EVENING GRATITUDE

A moment I protected my peace today:

_____

_____

TRUEJOY-LIVING

A YEAR OF TRANSFORMATION

DAY 229-Daily Devotion & Energetic Balance

"My body is a wise messenger."

MORNING RITUAL

Sit quietly and scan from head to toe.
Notice tension, warmth, energy.
Whisper: "I listen without judgment."

_____

_____

JOURNAL REFLECTION

What is my body communicating today?
How do I usually ignore its messages?
What does honoring my body look like daily?

_____

_____

MEAL & MOVEMENT

Eat what feels nourishing rather than habitual.
Move where the body calls — stretch, walk, rest.

Today I nourish my body with:

_____

Today I move with intention through:

_____

"My body is my ally."

EVENING GRATITUDE

A way I listened to my body:

_____

_____

DAY 230-Daily Devotion & Energetic Balance

"Rest is productive for the soul."

MORNING RITUAL

Plan a mid-day pause before the day begins.
Whisper: "I honor the natural ebb in my energy."
(Scheduling rest is self-respect, not laziness.)

MEAL & MOVEMENT

Eat soothing meals rich in minerals and hydration.
Move gently — slow stretch before naps or evening wind-down.

Today I nourish my body with:

_____

Today I move with intention through:

_____

JOURNAL REFLECTION

How do I define rest beyond sleep?
What makes me feel most restored?
How can I prioritize renewal without guilt?

_____

"I recharge with grace."

EVENING GRATITUDE

A moment of true rest today:

_____

_____

DAY 231–Daily Devotion & Energetic Balance

"Every action can be sacred."

MORNING RITUAL

Whisper: "May everything I do today be done with love."
Move through ordinary tasks with presence — washing dishes, working, speaking.
(Devotion is found in attention and intention.)

MEAL & MOVEMENT

Eat mindfully, thanking the earth for each ingredient. Move with reverence — yoga, walking meditation, or simply stretch with gratitude.

Today I nourish my body with:

_____

Today I move with intention through:

_____

JOURNAL REFLECTION

How can my daily routine become spiritual practice?
What makes an action feel holy?
How did love guide me today?

_____

"My life is a living prayer."

EVENING GRATITUDE
A moment I felt life as sacred:

_____

_____

DAY 232-Emotional Flow & Grace in Action

"Feeling is healing."

MORNING RITUAL

Place your hands on your chest. Whisper: "It's safe to feel."
As emotion arises today, breathe into it instead of resisting. Visualize energy flowing freely through your heart, cleansing you gently.
(This ritual builds emotional resilience through acceptance, not suppression.)

MEAL & MOVEMENT

Eat heart-nourishing foods — beets, leafy greens, herbal tea. Move fluidly — dance or stretch with emotion as movement.

Today I nourish my body with:

_____

Today I move with intention through:

_____

JOURNAL REFLECTION

What emotion asked for attention today?
How did I honor it?
How does feeling fully bring freedom?

_____

"My emotions are messengers of truth."

EVENING GRATITUDE
An emotion I allowed today:

_____

_____

DAY 233-Emotional Flow & Grace in Action

"Grace carries me through change."

MORNING RITUAL

Whisper: "I choose grace in every motion."
Move through your morning slowly — no rushing, no multitasking — letting each action feel intentional.
(Grace turns rhythm into ritual.)

JOURNAL REFLECTION

What does grace mean to me today?
How can I bring softness into my actions?
When have I experienced grace in chaos?

MEAL & MOVEMENT

Eat light, balanced meals. Move elegantly — flow yoga or walking with posture and poise.

Today I nourish my body with:

_____

Today I move with intention through:

_____

"Grace flows where effort ends."

EVENING GRATITUDE

A moment I moved with grace:

_____

_____

DAY 234—Emotional Flow & Grace in Action

"Connection nurtures my spirit."

MORNING RITUAL

Whisper: "I open my heart to meaningful connection."
Reach out to someone with presence — a message, a smile, a check-in.
(Human connection grounds energy into shared joy.)

MEAL & MOVEMENT

Share a meal with someone or eat mindfully while reflecting on loved ones. Move socially — walk or stretch with a friend.

Today I nourish my body with:

_____

Today I move with intention through:

_____

JOURNAL REFLECTION

Who brought warmth to my day?
How do I show up with presence in relationships?
What connections nourish me most?

_____

_____

"I am never alone; love surrounds me."

EVENING GRATITUDE
A connection that fed my soul today:

_____

_____

DAY 235-Emotional Flow & Grace in Action

"What I resist persists; what I allow transforms."

MORNING RITUAL

Whisper: "I surrender my need to control."
Notice where you tense or push today; soften those
areas with breath.
(Surrender creates spaciousness for miracles.)

MEAL & MOVEMENT

Eat simple, digestible meals. Move gently — focus
on releasing tight muscles or holding patterns.

Today I nourish my body with:

Today I move with intention through:

JOURNAL REFLECTION

Where am I holding tension emotionally or physically?
What happens when I stop fighting what is?
How can surrender feel empowering?

"I flow with life effortlessly."

EVENING GRATITUDE
Something I released today:

TRUEJOY-LIVING

A YEAR OF TRANSFORMATION

DAY 236-Emotional Flow & Grace in Action

"I am worthy of my own tenderness."

MORNING RITUAL

Look in the mirror and whisper:
"You're doing beautifully. I love you."
Offer yourself the same kindness you'd give to a friend.
(Compassion softens perfectionism into peace.)

MEAL & MOVEMENT

Eat comforting, warm meals. Move lovingly —
gentle yoga, self-massage, or stretching.

Today I nourish my body with:

_____

Today I move with intention through:

_____

JOURNAL REFLECTION

Where did I judge myself today?
What would compassion sound like instead?
How does gentleness change my inner voice?

"I am kind to my becoming."

EVENING GRATITUDE

A way I showed myself compassion today:

_____

DAY 237-Emotional Flow & Grace in Action

"Joy is my natural frequency."

MORNING RITUAL

Whisper: "Today I choose joy on purpose."

Seek one simple joy — sunlight, laughter, favorite music.

(Joy is not found; it's remembered.)

MEAL & MOVEMENT

Eat vibrant colors — fruits, greens, citrus.
Move playfully — dance, skip, or sway freely.

Today I nourish my body with:

Today I move with intention through:

JOURNAL REFLECTION

What sparks joy in my life right now?

How can I infuse joy into the ordinary?

What memories remind me of pure happiness?

"Joy is who I am."

EVENING GRATITUDE
A joyful moment from today:

DAY 238-Emotional Flow & Grace in Action

"Showing up is enough."

MORNING RITUAL

Whisper: "I release the need to get it right."
Today, notice where perfectionism tightens your
energy and replace it with permission to simply be.
(Presence outshines perfection.)

_____

_____

JOURNAL REFLECTION

Where did I strive for perfection today?
How does embracing presence lighten my energy?
What does "good enough" feel like to my soul?

_____

_____

MEAL & MOVEMENT

Eat naturally, without overthinking "should."
Move without metrics — enjoy the motion
itself.

Today I nourish my body with:

_____

Today I move with intention through:

_____

"Presence is my perfection."

EVENING GRATITUDE

A moment I released perfection:

_____

_____

DAY 239-Emotional Flow & Grace in Action

"I move at the pace of my peace."

MORNING RITUAL

Whisper: "I trust the timing of my life."
Today, honor your rhythm — rest when tired, move when inspired.
(Self-trust deepens through honoring natural pace.)

MEAL & MOVEMENT

Eat when truly hungry. Move intuitively — slower or faster depending on how your energy flows

Today I nourish my body with:

_____

Today I move with intention through:

_____

JOURNAL REFLECTION

What is my natural rhythm today?
How does ignoring it affect my well-being?
How can I align more closely with my inner pace?

_____

_____

"My timing is divine."

EVENING GRATITUDE

A moment I honored my rhythm:

_____

_____

DAY 240-Emotional Flow & Grace in Action

"I am grace in motion."

MORNING RITUAL

Whisper: "Thank you for the flow of this life."
Take a gratitude walk — breathing deeply, noticing
beauty around you.
(Gratitude transforms awareness into
embodiment.)

MEAL & MOVEMENT

Eat something you love slowly and mindfully.
Move gracefully — walking, stretching, or
gentle yoga with music.

Today I nourish my body with:

_____

Today I move with intention through:

_____

JOURNAL REFLECTION

What does flowing with grace mean to me now?
How has gratitude shaped my journey?
How can I live this flow daily?

"I live in gratitude, I move in grace."

EVENING GRATITUDE

A moment I felt grace today:

_____

_____

DAY 241-Living with Purpose & Service

"My purpose is expressed through how I show up."

MORNING RITUAL

Whisper: "May I move through today as love in action."

As you go about ordinary moments — working, cleaning, connecting — infuse awareness and compassion into each gesture.

(Purpose isn't found; it's lived through presence.)

MEAL & MOVEMENT

Eat intentionally — nourish your body to serve well. Move with calm focus — yoga, posture work, or mindful walking.

Today I nourish my body with:

_____

Today I move with intention through:

_____

JOURNAL REFLECTION

What feels most meaningful in my day-to-day life?

How can I serve through presence rather than performance?

Who benefits when I am fully present?

_____

_____

"Every moment lived with love fulfills my purpose."

EVENING GRATITUDE

A moment I lived my purpose through presence:

_____

_____

DAY 242-Living with Purpose & Service

"My light uplifts without effort."

MORNING RITUAL

Whisper: "I shine naturally by being myself."
Visualize a gentle golden glow radiating from your
heart — touching everyone you meet today.
(Inspiration happens through authenticity, not
striving.)

JOURNAL REFLECTION

When do I feel most radiant?
How does my energy affect others?
Where can I let my light shine more freely?

MEAL & MOVEMENT

Eat colorful, vibrant foods. Move expansively — open-
chest postures or dance to energize your light.

Today I nourish my body with:

Today I move with intention through:

"My light is love in motion."

EVENING GRATITUDE

A moment my light uplifted someone:

DAY 243-Living with Purpose & Service

"Integrity is my leadership."

MORNING RITUAL

Whisper: "May my actions teach louder than my words."
Notice opportunities to model presence, compassion, and calm in daily interactions.
(Leadership begins with alignment.)

MEAL & MOVEMENT

Eat balanced meals that sustain energy. Move intentionally — strong yet graceful postures.

Today I nourish my body with:

_____

Today I move with intention through:

_____

JOURNAL REFLECTION

What values guide my decisions today?
How can I embody them more visibly?
Who am I inspiring through consistency?

_____

"I lead through example and ease."

EVENING GRATITUDE

A moment I led with integrity:

_____

_____

DAY 244-Living with Purpose & Service

"I give from fullness, not fatigue."

MORNING RITUAL

Whisper: "I fill my own cup first."
Spend five minutes doing something that
replenishes you — breath, music, silence —
before serving others.
(Service rooted in self-care sustains impact.)

JOURNAL REFLECTION

How can I fill my cup before giving today?
What drains my energy when I serve?
What does balanced giving feel like?

MEAL & MOVEMENT

Eat nourishing, grounding meals. Move to recharge
— restorative yoga or walking outdoors.

Today I nourish my body with:

_____

Today I move with intention through:

_____

"I give joyfully from my overflow."

EVENING GRATITUDE

A moment I served from fullness:

_____

_____

DAY 245-Living with Purpose & Service

"My gifts are meant to be shared."

MORNING RITUAL

Whisper: "Today I share what comes naturally."
Offer your talents — creativity, listening, laughter — without expectation.
(Your gift blesses the world simply by being expressed.)

MEAL & MOVEMENT

Eat with community or connection. Move with joy — walking or light exercise that awakens gratitude.

Today I nourish my body with:

Today I move with intention through:

JOURNAL REFLECTION

What comes easily to me that serves others?
How can I express that more today?
How does giving freely expand my joy?

"My giving multiplies abundance."

EVENING GRATITUDE

A gift I shared today:

DAY 246-Living with Purpose & Service

"Meaning fuels my motivation."

MORNING RITUAL

Whisper: "I choose purpose over pressure."
Before starting tasks, ask: Does this align with
my values? Adjust your focus accordingly.
(Alignment replaces burnout with fulfillment.)

MEAL & MOVEMENT

Eat energizing, clear meals — greens, grains, hydration.
Move intentionally — mindful posture or standing
stretches at work.

Today I nourish my body with:

Today I move with intention through:

JOURNAL REFLECTION

What values matter most to me in my work or service?
Where do I feel most aligned — or off balance?
What one change could bring more integrity to my day?

"Purpose guides my path."

EVENING GRATITUDE

A way I aligned my work with meaning:

DAY 247-Living with Purpose & Service

"I am grateful to make a difference."

MORNING RITUAL

Whisper: "I serve with a grateful heart."
Reflect on the ripple your energy creates —
even small acts shift worlds.
(Humility honors both giving and receiving as
sacred exchange.)

JOURNAL REFLECTION

How did I contribute positively today?
Who or what did I uplift through my presence?
How can I stay humble yet proud of my service?

MEAL & MOVEMENT

Eat celebratory but balanced meals —
something you love. Move in gratitude —
walking or dancing as thanksgiving.

Today I nourish my body with:

Today I move with intention through:

"I am thankful to be a vessel of good."

EVENING GRATITUDE

A moment my service mattered:

DAY 248-Living Abundance & Contribution

"Abundance is the rhythm of my being."

MORNING RITUAL

Whisper: "I am already abundant."
Close your eyes and list everything that supports
your life right now — air, sunlight, relationships,
opportunities. Feel how full you already are.
(This ritual trains your nervous system to
recognize enoughness as your natural baseline.)

JOURNAL REFLECTION

Where do I already feel abundant?
What beliefs keep me from seeing my blessings?
How does gratitude attract more of what I desire?

MEAL & MOVEMENT

Eat colorfully — reflect abundance through variety.
Move expansively — open-body postures or deep
breathing outdoors.

Today I nourish my body with:

_____

Today I move with intention through:

_____

"I am open to infinite good."

EVENING GRATITUDE

Something abundant in my life today:

_____

_____

DAY 249-Living Abundance & Contribution

"What I give with joy returns multiplied."

MORNING RITUAL

Whisper: "Today, I give from love, not lack."
Offer kindness, time, or resources joyfully —
no expectation of return.
(Generosity affirms that you have more than
enough.)

JOURNAL REFLECTION

How does it feel to give freely?
What have I been withholding that I could share easily?
How does generosity shift my energy?

MEAL & MOVEMENT

Share a meal if possible. Move outward — walk,
volunteer, or simply smile at others intentionally.

Today I nourish my body with:

Today I move with intention through:

"I live in a flow of giving and receiving.

EVENING GRATITUDE

A moment I gave joyfully today:

DAY 250-Living Abundance & Contribution
"Gratitude is my magnet for miracles."

MORNING RITUAL

Whisper: "Thank you for the wealth that already surrounds me."

Write down three things you're grateful for financially or materially, then bless them with appreciation.

(Gratitude shifts scarcity into expansion instantly.)

_____

_____

JOURNAL REFLECTION

What am I grateful for that money can't buy?

How does gratitude change how I spend or share?

What blessings do I overlook most?

_____

_____

MEAL & MOVEMENT

Eat with gratitude — appreciate the labor and resources behind each bite. Move with abundance — full breaths, confident strides.

Today I nourish my body with:

_____

Today I move with intention through:

_____

"Gratitude grows my good."

EVENING GRATITUDE

A blessing I appreciated more deeply today:

_____

_____

DAY 251-Living Abundance & Contribution
"My creativity naturally enriches the world."

MORNING RITUAL

Whisper: "I am a vessel of creative flow."
Set the intention to create or express something small today — a note, an idea, an act of beauty. (Value creation flows when aligned with authenticity.)

MEAL & MOVEMENT

Eat energizing foods that spark creativity — citrus, nuts, green tea. Move dynamically — shake, stretch, or flow to open the body's channels.
Today I nourish my body with:

Today I move with intention through:

JOURNAL REFLECTION

What am I creating today?
How does creativity connect me to joy?
What comes easily to me that adds value to others?

"My creativity is infinite supply."

EVENING GRATITUDE

Something I created or contributed:

DAY 252-Living Abundance & Contribution

"Money flows easily when I am aligned."

MORNING RITUAL

Whisper: "I open my energy to receiving."
Visualize financial flow as water — abundant, clean, always circulating.
Smile as you imagine yourself within it.
(Abundance expands when met with joy and receptivity.)

MEAL & MOVEMENT

Eat foods that symbolize flow — soups, smoothies, teas. Move fluidly — flowing yoga or dancing with fluid motions.

Today I nourish my body with:

Today I move with intention through:

JOURNAL REFLECTION

How do I feel about receiving money or help?
What would it feel like to let it flow without fear?
How can I bless financial flow in and out?

"Money flows in harmony with my purpose."

EVENING GRATITUDE

A moment of receiving or prosperity today:

DAY 253-Living Abundance & Contribution

"What I bless expands — for them and for me."

MORNING RITUAL

Whisper: "I celebrate others' success as proof of possibility."
Send silent blessings to three people thriving in ways that inspire you.
(Celebration dissolves comparison and invites shared abundance.)

_____

_____

JOURNAL REFLECTION

Who can I celebrate today?
How does celebration expand my own abundance mindset?
What would it feel like to see success as shared energy?

_____

_____

MEAL & MOVEMENT

Eat something celebratory — your favorite fruit or dessert. Move with joy — dance or sway to uplifting music.

Today I nourish my body with:

_____

Today I move with intention through:

_____

"Blessing others blesses me."

EVENING GRATITUDE

Someone I celebrated today:

_____

_____

DAY 254–Living Abundance & Contribution

"I manage my blessings with wisdom and grace."

MORNING RITUAL

Whisper: "I honor what I have and where it flows."
Review your time, energy, and resources — gently realign them toward purpose and joy.
(Stewardship transforms abundance into sustainable flow.)

MEAL & MOVEMENT

Eat simple, nourishing meals. Move intentionally — posture, breathing, or walking that feels grounded in confidence.

Today I nourish my body with:

Today I move with intention through:

JOURNAL REFLECTION

How do I care for what I've been given?
Where can I manage with more mindfulness?
How can I use my abundance to serve others?

"I am a conscious steward of abundance."

EVENING GRATITUDE

A resource I used wisely today:

DAY 255-Purpose in Action — Work, Creativity & Calling

"Even the smallest task carries sacred purpose."

MORNING RITUAL

Whisper: "Whatever I do today, I will do with love."
Choose one ordinary activity — washing dishes, answering emails, driving — and do it with complete mindfulness.
(Purpose is born from intention, not importance.)

JOURNAL REFLECTION

How can I bring purpose into the ordinary?
What does "meaningful work" feel like to me?
How can small actions reflect big values?

MEAL & MOVEMENT

Eat mindfully — every bite a meditation in gratitude. Move intentionally — stretching or walking between tasks to refresh focus

Today I nourish my body with:

Today I move with intention through:

"Everything I touch becomes sacred through presence."

EVENING GRATITUDE
A task I infused with purpose today:

DAY 256-Purpose in Action — Work, Creativity & Calling

"Joy fuels my productivity and purpose."

MORNING RITUAL

Whisper: "I choose joy as my motivation."
Start your workday by setting one joyful intention
— a smile, music, or gratitude before beginning.
(Alignment with joy leads to inspired efficiency.)

MEAL & MOVEMENT

Eat energizing foods that lift mood — citrus, greens,
protein. Move to energize creativity — light cardio or
upbeat movement.

Today I nourish my body with:

_____

Today I move with intention through:

_____

JOURNAL REFLECTION

How does joy influence the quality of my work?
What small joys can I add to my routine?
When did I last feel truly inspired by what I do?

"Joy makes my work divine."

EVENING GRATITUDE

A joyful moment at work today:

_____

_____

DAY 257-Purpose in Action — Work, Creativity & Calling

"Inspiration becomes impact when I act in alignment."

MORNING RITUAL

Whisper: "I take one inspired action today."
Write down an idea you've delayed. Take one small, simple step toward it — a message, outline, or commitment.
(Momentum builds through alignment, not pressure.)

MEAL & MOVEMENT

Eat grounding foods for focus — whole grains, seeds, vegetables. Move with strength — core or stability exercises.

Today I nourish my body with:

Today I move with intention through:

JOURNAL REFLECTION

What inspired action did I take today?
How can I make progress through ease, not strain?
What idea keeps calling for expression?

"Aligned action amplifies my vision."

EVENING GRATITUDE

A step I took toward my dreams:

DAY 258-Purpose in Action — Work, Creativity & Calling

"Creativity flows through me effortlessly."

MORNING RITUAL

Whisper: "I am open to inspiration in all forms."
Set aside five minutes for pure creation — doodle,
write, sing, decorate, or brainstorm.
(Creativity thrives in play, not perfection.)

MEAL & MOVEMENT

Eat foods that stimulate the senses — fresh herbs, fruits,
spices. Move freely — dance or flow with intuitive rhythm.

Today I nourish my body with:

Today I move with intention through:

JOURNAL REFLECTION

What inspires me creatively right now?
How can I nurture creativity without judgment?
What environments spark my best ideas?

"I am a channel for divine creativity."

EVENING GRATITUDE

Something I created today:

TRUEJOY-LIVING

A YEAR OF TRANSFORMATION

DAY 259-Purpose in Action — Work, Creativity & Calling

"Together, we create more than we can alone."

MORNING RITUAL

Whisper: "I welcome connection in co-creation."
Today, listen more than you speak. See others'
perspectives as invitations to expand, not compete.
(Collaboration is the sacred art of mutual
expansion.)

MEAL & MOVEMENT

Eat shared or family-style if possible. Move cooperatively
— group walks, classes, or synchronized flow.

Today I nourish my body with:

Today I move with intention through:

JOURNAL REFLECTION

How does collaboration enhance my creativity?
Where can I release control and trust synergy?
Who inspires me to grow through teamwork?

"I thrive through connection."

EVENING GRATITUDE

A collaborative moment that uplifted me:

DAY 260-Purpose in Action — Work, Creativity & Calling

"Steady steps create lasting growth."

MORNING RITUAL

Whisper: "I trust the process of progress."
As challenges arise, breathe deeply and repeat the
mantra: "Slow is smooth, smooth is steady."
(Patience converts persistence into peace.)

MEAL & MOVEMENT

Eat steadying meals — protein, grains, water. Move at a
deliberate pace — slow strength training, mindful walking.

Today I nourish my body with:

_____

Today I move with intention through:

_____

JOURNAL REFLECTION

Where do I need patience in my work or dreams?
How can I measure success by growth, not speed?
What has consistency taught me so far?

"My timing is divine."

_____

EVENING GRATITUDE

A moment I stayed patient today:

_____

_____

DAY 261-Purpose in Action — Work, Creativity & Calling

"Every step forward is a victory."

MORNING RITUAL

Whisper: "I honor how far I've come."
Review your week, noticing wins both big and
small. Smile at your progress.
(Acknowledgment reinforces alignment.)

MEAL & MOVEMENT

Eat your favorite celebratory meal. Move playfully —
dance, stretch, or walk while smiling with gratitude.

Today I nourish my body with:

_____

Today I move with intention through:

_____

JOURNAL REFLECTION

What progress am I proud of this week?
How can I celebrate consistency over outcomes?
What does "enough" feel like today?

"Progress is perfection in motion."

EVENING GRATITUDE

Something I'm proud of accomplishing:

_____

DAY 262-Leadership Through Presence & Impact

"My presence inspires more than my title ever could."

MORNING RITUAL

Whisper: "May my energy lead the way."
Today, before you speak or act, pause and ground.
Lead from calm energy, not urgency.
(True leadership begins with self-regulation.)

MEAL & MOVEMENT

Eat grounding foods — oats, lentils, roots. Move confidently — shoulders back, deep breathing, strong posture.

Today I nourish my body with:

_____

Today I move with intention through:

_____

JOURNAL REFLECTION

How does my energy influence others?
What would it feel like to lead quietly but powerfully?
How can I embody calm confidence today?

_____

_____

"My energy leads with love."

EVENING GRATITUDE

A moment I led through calm presence:

_____

_____

DAY 263-Leadership Through Presence & Impact

"Listening is the language of connection."

MORNING RITUAL

Whisper: "Today I will listen with my heart."

During each conversation, focus fully.

Listen not to reply, but to feel.

(Empathetic listening builds trust and unity.)

MEAL & MOVEMENT

Eat quietly — no screens, just savor. Move slowly — walk or stretch mindfully while noticing sound and silence.

Today I nourish my body with:

_____

Today I move with intention through:

_____

JOURNAL REFLECTION

When do I listen deeply, and when do I rush to respond?

How does true listening change relationships?

Who needs my full attention today?

"Listening connects me to love."

EVENING GRATITUDE

A moment of true understanding today:

_____

_____

DAY 264-Leadership Through Presence & Impact

My words heal, connect, and uplift."

MORNING RITUAL

Whisper: "I speak from clarity and kindness."
Before responding to tension, breathe once, then
choose words that soothe rather than sting.
(Compassionate communication sustains harmony in
all forms of leadership.)

MEAL & MOVEMENT

Eat calmly — warm tea or soup to soothe the throat
chakra. Move with openness — chest stretches, gentle
flows.

Today I nourish my body with:

_____

Today I move with intention through:

_____

JOURNAL REFLECTION

How can I speak more lovingly under stress?
What does compassionate honesty look like?
What conversations deserve gentleness today?

My words are bridges of peace."

EVENING GRATITUDE

A moment I communicated with love:

_____

_____

DAY 265-Leadership Through Presence & Impact

"I lift others by believing in their light."

MORNING RITUAL

Whisper: "May my encouragement awaken someone's courage."
Today, compliment or affirm at least one person sincerely.
(Empowerment is the highest form of leadership.)

MEAL & MOVEMENT

Eat vibrant foods that uplift mood. Move outward — walks or shared activities that foster connection.

Today I nourish my body with:

Today I move with intention through:

JOURNAL REFLECTION

Who can I encourage today?
How does empowering others strengthen me?
What does "leading through love" mean to me?

"Empowerment multiplies energy."

EVENING GRATITUDE

Someone I encouraged today:

DAY 266-Leadership Through Presence & Impact

"Success deepens my humility and gratitude."

MORNING RITUAL

Whisper: "I receive success with grace."
Celebrate wins without attachment — gratitude
keeps your feet on the ground as you rise.
(Grounded success remains sustainable.)

MEAL & MOVEMENT

Eat nourishing, stable meals — proteins and roots.
Move slowly — strong grounding postures or walks
in nature.

Today I nourish my body with:

_____

Today I move with intention through:

_____

JOURNAL REFLECTION

What success have I recently achieved?
How can I celebrate without ego?
How can I stay humble and grateful in growth?

_____

_____

"Gratitude roots my achievements."

EVENING GRATITUDE

A success I appreciated with humility:

_____

_____

DAY 267-Leadership Through Presence & Impact

"My truth is my greatest influence."

MORNING RITUAL

Whisper: "I inspire by being real."
Let go of roles or personas — show up as your whole, imperfect self today.
(Authenticity magnetizes trust and connection.)

MEAL & MOVEMENT

Eat naturally — foods close to the earth. Move organically — no structure, just intuitive flow.

Today I nourish my body with:

_____

Today I move with intention through:

_____

JOURNAL REFLECTION

Where am I still hiding behind an image?
What truth about me inspires others most?
How can I show more humanity in my leadership?

"My truth is powerful and kind."

EVENING GRATITUDE

A moment of authentic expression today:

_____

_____

DAY 268-Leadership Through Presence & Impact

"Love is my legacy."

MORNING RITUAL

Whisper: "May everything I lead begin and end in love."
Throughout the day, pause before each decision and ask: "Is this rooted in love or fear?"
Choose love. Always.
(Love-centered leadership leaves lasting impact.)

JOURNAL REFLECTION

How does leading with love change my world?
What does love-based leadership feel like in my body?
How can I model this energy in every role I play?

MEAL & MOVEMENT

Eat comforting, heart-centered foods. Move rhythmically — flowing movements that mirror an open heart.

Today I nourish my body with:

Today I move with intention through:

"I lead with love, always."

EVENING GRATITUDE
A moment I chose love over fear:

TRUEJOY-LIVING
A YEAR OF TRANSFORMATION

DAY 269-Returning to Joy & Simplicity

"Joy is the language of my soul."

MORNING RITUAL

Whisper: "Today I choose simplicity."
Do one small thing that delights your senses — sip tea slowly, feel sunshine, listen to music.
(Simplicity clears space for joy to bloom.)

MEAL & MOVEMENT

Eat your favorite simple meal — one that feels like comfort. Move playfully — dance, sway, or stroll with lightness.

Today I nourish my body with:

Today I move with intention through:

JOURNAL REFLECTION

What brings me natural joy?
How can I make space for more of it?
Where can I simplify today?

"Joy is always here when I slow down."

EVENING GRATITUDE

A simple joy I felt today:

DAY 270-Returning to Joy & Simplicity

"Now is where my peace lives."

MORNING RITUAL

Whisper: "I savor each breath, each step."
Throughout the day, pause and name one thing you
can see, hear, and feel.
(Mindful savoring turns ordinary life into
ceremony.)

MEAL & MOVEMENT

Eat slowly, tasting every bite. Move with awareness
— feel each muscle as it lengthens and releases.

Today I nourish my body with:

_____

Today I move with intention through:

_____

JOURNAL REFLECTION

What moments did I truly experience today?
How does presence change my perception of time?
Where do I rush past life's sweetness?

"Presence is my home."

_____

EVENING GRATITUDE

A moment I savored fully:

_____

_____

DAY 271-Returning to Joy & Simplicity

"Laughter is medicine for my spirit."

MORNING RITUAL

Whisper: "Today, I welcome lightness."
Watch or recall something that makes you laugh. Let
the sound vibrate through your chest.
(Joy heals by reminding us we're alive.)

JOURNAL REFLECTION

What made me laugh today?
How can I take life a little less seriously?
What does lightheartedness feel like in my body?

MEAL & MOVEMENT

Eat something fun — colorful fruits or a favorite treat.
Move playfully — dance or stretch with a smile.

Today I nourish my body with:

Today I move with intention through:

"Lightness lifts me higher."

EVENING GRATITUDE

A moment of laughter I cherished:

DAY 272–Returning to Joy & Simplicity

"Who I am and what I have is enough."

MORNING RITUAL

Whisper: "I release striving and rest in sufficiency."
As you breathe, imagine soft golden energy
surrounding you — contentment embodied.
(Enoughness is the quiet luxury of the soul.)

MEAL & MOVEMENT

Eat nourishing comfort foods. Move gently — restorative
yoga or slow walking.

Today I nourish my body with:

_____

Today I move with intention through:

_____

JOURNAL REFLECTION

Where do I still chase "more"?
How can I honor contentment today?
What if enough was already here?

"Contentment is my true abundance."

EVENING GRATITUDE

A moment I felt enough:

_____

_____

DAY 273-Returning to Joy & Simplicity

"Peace is my natural tempo."

MORNING RITUAL

Whisper: "I move at the pace of peace."
Structure your day with gentle rhythm — breaks for breath, meals, and rest.
(Peaceful pacing builds sustained energy and grace.)

MEAL & MOVEMENT

Eat balanced meals at consistent times. Move in flow — tai chi, stretching, or walking meditation.

Today I nourish my body with:

_____

Today I move with intention through:

_____

JOURNAL REFLECTION

How does my pace feel today?
Where can I slow down?
What rhythm supports my wellbeing?

"I walk to the beat of serenity."

EVENING GRATITUDE

A peaceful rhythm I honored:

_____

_____

DAY 274-Returning to Joy & Simplicity

"Beauty awakens gratitude in my soul."

MORNING RITUAL

Whisper: "I open my eyes to wonder."
Notice beauty in one detail — a flower, a sound, a smile — and let gratitude ripple through you.
(Beauty is the sacred mirror of divine joy.)

MEAL & MOVEMENT

Eat visually beautiful food — colorful bowls, fresh fruit. Move gracefully — dance, paint, or stretch aesthetically.

Today I nourish my body with:

Today I move with intention through:

JOURNAL REFLECTION

What beauty touched me today?

How do I define beauty beyond appearance?

How can I bring more of it into my environment?

"Beauty lives in everything I see."

EVENING GRATITUDE

A beautiful moment I noticed:

DAY 275-Returning to Joy & Simplicity

"Ease is my expression of trust."

MORNING RITUAL

Whisper: "I release tension and move in grace."
Take three long exhales, letting your shoulders drop.
(Ease is not laziness — it's alignment in motion.)

MEAL & MOVEMENT

Eat lightly and joyfully. Move slowly — yoga, walking, or gentle flow that feels effortless.

Today I nourish my body with:

_____

Today I move with intention through:

_____

JOURNAL REFLECTION

Where can I replace effort with ease?
How does relaxing into trust change my results?
What would an ease-filled life look like?

"Ease is my natural way of being."

EVENING GRATITUDE
A moment of ease I felt today:

_____

_____

DAY 276-Living Radiantly —
Harmony, Wonder & Heart-Led Flow.
"My light glows naturally when I live in truth."

MORNING RITUAL

Whisper: "Today I let my inner light lead."
Stand near sunlight or imagine golden light filling
your chest.
Inhale radiance, exhale self-consciousness.
(Radiance is the effortless glow of authenticity.)

MEAL & MOVEMENT

Eat light, colorful meals. Move with gentle strength
— yoga, stretching, or a walk that lets your energy
expand.

Today I nourish my body with:

_____

Today I move with intention through:

_____

_____

JOURNAL REFLECTION

What makes me feel most radiant?
When do I dim my own light?
How can I shine with ease, not effort?

_____

"I am radiant by nature."

EVENING GRATITUDE

A moment I glowed naturally today:

_____

_____

DAY 277-Living Radiantly —
Harmony, Wonder & Heart-Led Flow.

"My heart leads me in love and balance."

MORNING RITUAL

Whisper: "Heart, show me the way today."
Place both hands over your heart. Feel its rhythm. Ask:
"What do you need from me right now?"
Listen quietly.
(Harmony begins when the mind bows to the wisdom of the heart.)

JOURNAL REFLECTION

What is my heart guiding me toward?
How can I listen more deeply to my emotions?
Where do I need to lead with compassion?

MEAL & MOVEMENT

Eat heart-nourishing foods — berries, greens, teas. Move with rhythm — breath to heartbeat pace.

Today I nourish my body with:

_____

Today I move with intention through:

_____

"My heart is my compass."

EVENING GRATITUDE

A moment I followed my heart today:

_____

_____

_____

DAY 278-Living Radiantly —
Harmony, Wonder & Heart-Led Flow.

"Joy multiplies when I notice it."

MORNING RITUAL

Whisper: "Today I celebrate the ordinary."
Each time you feel gratitude, pause — smile, breathe,
and say "thank you" aloud.
(Tiny celebrations cultivate lasting joy.)

MEAL & MOVEMENT

Eat what feels festive — vibrant colors or favorite flavors.
Move playfully — sway, dance, or skip a little.

Today I nourish my body with:

_____

Today I move with intention through:

_____

JOURNAL REFLECTION

What small moments made me smile today?
How can I make celebration part of every day?
What tiny joys can I share with others?

_____

"Every joy, no matter how small, matters."

EVENING GRATITUDE

A small joy I celebrated:

_____

DAY 279-Living Radiantly —
Harmony, Wonder & Heart-Led Flow.
"Wonder keeps my spirit young."

MORNING RITUAL

Whisper: "I look at life through new eyes."
Find one thing you see every day — a tree, a cloud,
a mirror — and study it as if for the first time.
(Wonder reawakens presence.)

MEAL & MOVEMENT

Eat something new or in a new way. Move
curiously — explore a new path, routine, or
song.

Today I nourish my body with:

_____

Today I move with intention through:

_____

JOURNAL REFLECTION

What filled me with wonder today?
How does curiosity change my energy?
What am I ready to rediscover?

_____

"Wonder keeps my light alive."

EVENING GRATITUDE
Something that amazed me today:

_____

_____

DAY 280-Living Radiantly —
Harmony, Wonder & Heart-Led Flow.
"Self-care is how I protect my light."

MORNING RITUAL

Whisper: "I tend to myself with love today."
Choose one self-care act — skincare, journaling,
stretching — not as obligation, but devotion.
(When you care for yourself, you care for your
connection to Source.)

_____

_____

JOURNAL REFLECTION

How can I better care for my energy today?
What self-care ritual most soothes my soul?
How do I feel when I glow from within?

_____

_____

MEAL & MOVEMENT

Eat hydrating, nourishing foods — greens, soups,
water. Move gently — walks, restorative yoga, or
slow stretching.

Today I nourish my body with:

_____

Today I move with intention through:

_____

"Caring for myself keeps my light steady."

EVENING GRATITUDE

A moment I honored my energy:

_____

_____

DAY 281-Living Radiantly —
Harmony, Wonder & Heart-Led Flow.

"Life moves through me in perfect rhythm."

MORNING RITUAL

Whisper: "I dance with life today."
Play music that mirrors your mood. Let your body
move freely — no choreography, only feeling.
(Movement restores connection to life's melody.)

MEAL & MOVEMENT

Eat in rhythm — slow, steady bites. Move intuitively to
music at least once today.

Today I nourish my body with:

_____

Today I move with intention through:

_____

JOURNAL REFLECTION

What rhythm is life moving at for me right now?
How can I dance with change instead of resisting
it?
What song could represent my season of life?

_____

"I am in tune with life's harmony."

EVENING GRATITUDE

A moment I moved in flow today:

_____

DAY 282-Living Radiantly —
Harmony, Wonder & Heart-Led Flow.

"My presence is love made visible."

MORNING RITUAL

Whisper: "May everyone who crosses my path feel love."

Smile softly to yourself and imagine your heart expanding with each inhale.

(You are the walking expression of the love you've cultivated all year.)

MEAL & MOVEMENT

Eat foods that nourish warmth — soups, teas, spices.
Move with an open heart — chest open, shoulders soft.

Today I nourish my body with:

Today I move with intention through:

JOURNAL REFLECTION

How did I express love through presence today?
What does radiating love look like in daily life?
How has love shaped my transformation?

"I am love in motion."

EVENING GRATITUDE

A moment I shared love today:

DAY 283-Embodied Peace – Serenity, Trust & Wholeness.

"I protect my peace above all else."

MORNING RITUAL

Whisper: "Peace is my highest priority."
Visualize a serene bubble of calm light surrounding you. Any chaos that approaches softens and dissolves.
(You are allowed to be calm even when the world is not.)

JOURNAL REFLECTION

What steals my peace most often?
How can I respond differently next time?
What boundaries protect my serenity?

MEAL & MOVEMENT

Eat soothing meals — soups, teas, gentle flavors. Move to release tension — light yoga or deep, slow stretching.

Today I nourish my body with:

Today I move with intention through:

"Peace is my superpower."

EVENING GRATITUDE

A moment I chose peace today:

DAY 284-Embodied Peace – Serenity, Trust & Wholeness.

"Everything unfolds at the perfect pace."

MORNING RITUAL

Whisper: "I release the need to rush."
Visualize a river — smooth, steady, unstoppable.
You are floating peacefully, trusting the current.
(Trust turns waiting into alignment.)

MEAL & MOVEMENT

Eat in rhythm — slow, mindful bites. Move fluidly —
flowing yoga or mindful walking.

Today I nourish my body with:

_____

Today I move with intention through:

_____

JOURNAL REFLECTION

Where am I still trying to control timing?
How can I surrender more deeply to divine order?
What would it feel like to truly trust the process?

_____

_____

"My timing is divine."

EVENING GRATITUDE

A moment I trusted the flow:

_____

_____

DAY 285-Embodied Peace – Serenity, Trust & Wholeness.

"My body remembers peace."

MORNING RITUAL

Whisper: "With each breath, I return to safety."
Do 3 minutes of slow, conscious breathing —
inhaling calm, exhaling tension.
(Your body becomes your temple of tranquility.)

MEAL & MOVEMENT

Eat grounding meals — root vegetables, warm grains. Move gently — grounding postures or barefoot walking.

Today I nourish my body with:

_____

Today I move with intention through:

_____

JOURNAL REFLECTION

Where do I hold tension?
What practices bring me back to calm?
How does my body feel when I am truly peaceful?

_____

_____

"Peace lives in my breath."

EVENING GRATITUDE

A sensation of peace in my body:

_____

_____

DAY 286-Embodied Peace – Serenity, Trust & Wholeness.

"Acceptance sets me free."

MORNING RITUAL

Whisper: "I meet this moment as it is."
Repeat the phrase "This too is part of my journey"
whenever something unexpected arises today.
(Acceptance transforms resistance into grace.)

MEAL & MOVEMENT

Eat simply. Move gently — flow with whatever pace your
body needs today.

Today I nourish my body with:

Today I move with intention through:

JOURNAL REFLECTION

What have I been resisting?
How can I make peace with it instead?
What wisdom does acceptance reveal?

"Peace begins where resistance ends."

EVENING GRATITUDE
A situation I accepted today:

DAY 287-Embodied Peace – Serenity, Trust & Wholeness.

"Nothing is missing; I am whole."

MORNING RITUAL

Whisper: "Every part of me belongs."
Imagine gathering all versions of yourself — past, present, and future — and embracing them in light.
(Wholeness means loving yourself without condition.)

MEAL & MOVEMENT

Eat balanced meals. Move with intention — slow yoga or meditative breathing.

Today I nourish my body with:

_____

Today I move with intention through:

_____

JOURNAL REFLECTION

What part of me needs more love?
How can I integrate rather than fix?
What does wholeness feel like in my body?

_____

"I am already whole."

EVENING GRATITUDE

A part of myself I embraced today:

_____

_____

DAY 288-Embodied Peace – Serenity, Trust & Wholeness.

"Mystery is my ally."

MORNING RITUAL

Whisper: "I relax into the unknown."
When your mind seeks control, place a hand over your heart and repeat: "I am safe even without all the answers."
(Faith is peace in motion.)

JOURNAL REFLECTION

What do I still try to figure out or fix?
How can I trust mystery as part of magic?
How does surrender feel in my body?

MEAL & MOVEMENT

Eat intuitively — what your body asks for. Move softly — slow stretches or calming breathwork.

Today I nourish my body with:

Today I move with intention through:

"The unknown is sacred space."

EVENING GRATITUDE

Something I surrendered today:

DAY 289-Embodied Peace – Serenity, Trust & Wholeness.

"Stillness is my strength."

MORNING RITUAL

Whisper: "I find power in my pause."
Sit in silence for 5 minutes — focus only on the breath and heartbeat. Let thoughts drift away.
(In stillness, your true self speaks softly.)

JOURNAL REFLECTION

What does stillness reveal to me?
How can I bring silence into my day?
Where does stillness give me strength?

MEAL & MOVEMENT

Eat light, calming meals. Move meditatively — seated stretching, slow yoga, or still reflection.

Today I nourish my body with:

_____

Today I move with intention through:

_____

"Stillness renews my soul."

EVENING GRATITUDE

A peaceful pause I embraced:

_____

_____

DAY 290-Embodied Joy — Celebration, Expression & Connection

"Every step I've taken has led me home."

MORNING RITUAL

Whisper: "Today, I celebrate how far I've come."
Review one page of your journey — whether from
this planner, your memory, or your heart — and
acknowledge your growth.
(Celebration anchors transformation into
embodiment.)

MEAL & MOVEMENT

Eat a favorite celebratory meal. Move freely —
dance, stretch, or walk with joy.

Today I nourish my body with:

Today I move with intention through:

JOURNAL REFLECTION

What progress fills me with pride?
How can I celebrate myself with love, not ego?
What does celebration feel like in my body?

"I am proud of my becoming."

EVENING GRATITUDE

A moment I celebrated myself today:

DAY 291-Embodied Joy — Celebration, Expression & Connection

"Authentic expression is my liberation."

MORNING RITUAL

Whisper: "I speak my truth with love."
Sing, write, or move in a way that expresses how you feel today — no filter, just flow.
(Expression clears emotional energy and opens creative flow.)

_____

_____

JOURNAL REFLECTION

What truth wants to be expressed today?
How does expression bring me peace?
Where can I speak or create more freely?

_____

_____

MEAL & MOVEMENT

Eat bright, sensory foods — colorful veggies, spices. Move expressively — free dance, journaling, or art-making.

Today I nourish my body with:

_____

Today I move with intention through:

_____

"My voice is my freedom"

EVENING GRATITUDE
Something I expressed authentically today:

_____

_____

DAY 292-Embodied Joy — Celebration, Expression & Connection

"Heartfelt connection nourishes my soul."

MORNING RITUAL

Whisper: "May my heart meet others with compassion today."

Take one moment to reach out — a message, hug, or kind word that comes from true care.

(Connection is the highest form of joy in motion.)

JOURNAL REFLECTION

Who made me feel seen today?

How can I connect with more sincerity?

What relationships bring me genuine joy?

MEAL & MOVEMENT

Eat with someone you love, or share a meal virtually. Move socially — walk, stretch, or chat with connection.

Today I nourish my body with:

Today I move with intention through:

"Love connects me to all things."

EVENING GRATITUDE

A connection that warmed my heart:

DAY 293-Embodied Joy — Celebration, Expression & Connection

"My vulnerability is my beauty."

MORNING RITUAL

Whisper: "It's safe for me to be seen as I am."
Share something true — a feeling, story, or dream
— without editing or apology.
(Authentic visibility is an act of courage.)

MEAL & MOVEMENT

Eat comfort foods that nurture safety. Move gently —
opening postures for the chest and shoulders.

Today I nourish my body with:

Today I move with intention through:

JOURNAL REFLECTION

Where have I been hiding parts of myself?
What does it feel like to be truly seen?
How can I honor visibility as self-love?

"I am radiant in my truth."

EVENING GRATITUDE

A moment I allowed myself to be seen:

TRUEJOY-LIVING

A YEAR OF TRANSFORMATION

DAY 294-Embodied Joy — Celebration, Expression & Connection

"My joy is a gift that multiplies when shared."

MORNING RITUAL

Whisper: "Today, I'll let my joy ripple outward."
Smile at strangers, send gratitude messages, or
compliment someone genuinely.
(Joy is contagious energy that heals communities.)

MEAL & MOVEMENT

Eat foods you love — and share them if possible. Move
outwardly — group exercise, dancing, or playful walking.

Today I nourish my body with:

_____

Today I move with intention through:

_____

JOURNAL REFLECTION

How did I share joy today?
What was the reaction of others?
How did giving joy deepen my own?

"I am a fountain of joy."

EVENING GRATITUDE

A moment my joy touched someone:

_____

_____

DAY 295-Embodied Joy — Celebration, Expression & Connection

"Every moment holds magic when I'm present."

MORNING RITUAL

Whisper: "Today, I walk in reverence."
Treat ordinary actions — brushing teeth, making breakfast — as rituals of gratitude.
(The sacred hides in the simple.)

MEAL & MOVEMENT

Eat consciously — bless your food before each meal.
Move meditatively — walk with awareness or stretch in gratitude.

Today I nourish my body with:

Today I move with intention through:

JOURNAL REFLECTION

What simple act felt sacred today?
How can I bring ritual to my routine?
What moments remind me that life itself is holy?

"I live in continuous reverence."

EVENING GRATITUDE

A sacred moment I noticed:

DAY 296-Embodied Joy — Celebration, Expression & Connection

"I don't need to do to deserve joy."

MORNING RITUAL

Whisper: "I am enough exactly as I am."
Spend the first few minutes of your morning in quiet presence — no agenda, just breath and awareness.
(Joy exists in being, not achieving.)

MEAL & MOVEMENT

Eat intuitively — choose what feels nourishing. Move slowly, honoring how your body wants to flow.

Today I nourish my body with:

_____

Today I move with intention through:

_____

JOURNAL REFLECTION

What does joy feel like in stillness?
How can I rest without guilt?
What happens when I stop striving and simply exist?

"My joy is effortless presence."

EVENING GRATITUDE

A moment I enjoyed just being:

_____

TRUEJOY-LIVING

A YEAR OF TRANSFORMATION

DAY 297-Living as Light —
Purpose, Presence & Legacy
"My light makes the world brighter just by being."

MORNING RITUAL

Whisper: "Today, I'll let my light be seen."
Light a candle or stand in the sun.
Visualize your heart glowing and expanding to fill
the space around you.
(Illumination isn't loud — it's consistent presence.)

JOURNAL REFLECTION

Where in my life do I naturally shine?
How does my presence influence others?
What reminds me that my light is needed?

MEAL & MOVEMENT

Eat bright, colorful meals — think citrus, greens,
berries. Move openly — arms wide, chest lifted,
shoulders soft.

Today I nourish my body with:

Today I move with intention through:

"My light is my gift.

EVENING GRATITUDE

A moment I shone with love today:

TRUEJOY-LIVING
A YEAR OF TRANSFORMATION

DAY 298-Living as Light —
Purpose, Presence & Legacy

"My legacy is built through daily love."

MORNING RITUAL

Whisper: "Every act of kindness shapes my legacy."
Do one generous act today — big or small —
without expecting anything back.
(Legacy is simply love made visible through time.)

MEAL & MOVEMENT

Eat whole, hearty foods that sustain strength. Move
with intention — walk tall, steady, and grounded.

Today I nourish my body with:

_____

Today I move with intention through:

_____

JOURNAL REFLECTION

What impact do I hope to leave behind?
How am I already living that legacy?
Who am I becoming through my daily choices?

"I live my legacy moment by moment."

EVENING GRATITUDE

A legacy-building action I took today:

_____

_____

DAY 299-Living as Light —
Purpose, Presence & Legacy
"My calm energy uplifts every space I enter."

MORNING RITUAL

Whisper: "My presence is peace."
Before you speak or act, take one deep breath to center.
Notice how stillness naturally invites harmony.
(Presence is silent inspiration.)

JOURNAL REFLECTION

How do I inspire through simply being?
What energy do I bring into rooms?
How can I radiate calm without words?

MEAL & MOVEMENT

Eat balanced, peaceful meals. Move meditatively — walking, breathing, or gentle flow with awareness.

Today I nourish my body with:

_____

Today I move with intention through:

_____

"I lead by being."

EVENING GRATITUDE

A moment my presence made a difference:`

_____

_____

DAY 300-Living as Light —
Purpose, Presence & Legacy
"Love leads, and I follow."

MORNING RITUAL

Whisper: "May love be my compass today."
Before making decisions, pause and ask: "Is this love or fear?" — then act from love.
(Love-based action realigns the world toward wholeness.)

_____

_____

JOURNAL REFLECTION

What would love do in this situation?
How does love feel in my body when I act from it?
How can I be a vessel of unconditional love today?

_____

_____

MEAL & MOVEMENT

Eat heart-warming meals — soups, teas, comfort foods. Move with devotion — yoga, slow stretching, or mindful breath.

Today I nourish my body with:

_____

Today I move with intention through:

_____

_____

"Love is my way home."

EVENING GRATITUDE

A choice I made from love today:

_____

_____

DAY 301-Living as Light —
Purpose, Presence & Legacy
"What flows through me was meant to be shared."

MORNING RITUAL

Whisper: "I am a channel for good."
Share one gift — creativity, insight, laughter,
support — without expectation.
(True giving renews both giver and receiver.)

MEAL & MOVEMENT

Eat generously — prepare extra and offer some.
Move outwardly — group activities or shared flow.

Today I nourish my body with:

Today I move with intention through:

JOURNAL REFLECTION

What is one gift I shared today?
How does giving freely expand me?
How can I honor my gifts daily?

"Generosity is my joy."

EVENING GRATITUDE

A gift I gave or received today:

DAY 302-Living as Light —
Purpose, Presence & Legacy

"Wherever I go, I bring peace with me."

MORNING RITUAL

Whisper: "My steps are prayers of peace."
Walk mindfully — each step a blessing to the
ground and all beings.
(Your embodied peace is activism in its purest
form.)

MEAL & MOVEMENT

Eat harmonizing foods — greens, herbal tea. Move
rhythmically — slow walking or mindful stretching.

Today I nourish my body with:

Today I move with intention through:

JOURNAL REFLECTION

How can I create peace in small ways today?
Where can I bring gentleness into chaos?
How can I model calm strength for others?

"I am the peace I wish to see."

EVENING GRATITUDE

A moment I embodied peace:

DAY 303-Living as Light —
Purpose, Presence & Legacy

"I am connected to everything in love."

MORNING RITUAL

Whisper: "I am part of the infinite whole."
Close your eyes and feel the invisible web of connection — people, places, nature, energy — all pulsing as one heartbeat.
(Unity consciousness births compassion and purpose.)

MEAL & MOVEMENT

Eat from gratitude for Earth — plant-based or local foods. Move connectedly — outdoor breathing, barefoot grounding.

Today I nourish my body with:

Today I move with intention through:

JOURNAL REFLECTION

When do I feel most connected to all life?
How does unity shift how I treat others?
What truth does oneness reveal to me?

"I am part of everything, and everything is part of me."

EVENING GRATITUDE

A moment I felt oneness today:

DAY 304-Integration & Return —
Living TrueJoy Daily
"What I once practiced, I now embody."

MORNING RITUAL

Whisper: "Today, I live my alignment naturally."
Move through your morning rituals with ease — no checklist, just flow.
(You've become the calm you used to seek.)

MEAL & MOVEMENT

Eat your grounding go-to meal. Move the way your body asks — trusting your rhythm.

Today I nourish my body with:

_____

Today I move with intention through:

_____

JOURNAL REFLECTION

Which rituals now feel natural to me?
What has become second nature in my growth?
How does it feel to live in alignment?

_____

"I live what I know."

EVENING GRATITUDE
A moment I embodied my practice:

_____

DAY 305-Integration & Return —
Living TrueJoy Daily
"Gratitude is how I honor my journey."

MORNING RITUAL

Whisper: "I thank every lesson, every step."
(Reflection deepens integration.)

MEAL & MOVEMENT

Eat slowly, savoring textures. Move reflectively — slow yoga, walking, or stretching.

Today I nourish my body with:

_____

Today I move with intention through:

_____

JOURNAL REFLECTION

What am I most grateful for this year?
How have I changed?
What am I still learning to receive?

"Gratitude completes every cycle."

EVENING GRATITUDE
A lesson I'm thankful for:

_____

_____

DAY 306-Integration & Return —
Living TrueJoy Daily
"Each season serves my growth."

MORNING RITUAL

Whisper: "I honor where I am."
Reflect on your current season — is it
rest, creativity, expansion, or healing?
Accept it fully.
(Peace blooms through cyclical
awareness.)

_____

_____

JOURNAL REFLECTION

What season am I in right now?
What wisdom is it teaching me?
How can I work with it, not against it?

_____

_____

MEAL & MOVEMENT

Eat seasonally. Move gently — nature walk, light flow, or
grounding poses.

Today I nourish my body with:

_____

Today I move with intention through:

_____

"Each phase brings grace."

EVENING GRATITUDE

Something my current season has taught me:

_____

_____

TRUEJOY-LIVING
A YEAR OF TRANSFORMATION

DAY 307-Integration & Return —
Living TrueJoy Daily

"Balance is the art of my joy."

MORNING RITUAL

Whisper: "Today I flow with balance."
Alternate between gentle action and
quiet pause — work, then breathe.
(Balance creates sustainable energy.)

_____

_____

MEAL & MOVEMENT

Eat evenly balanced meals. Move in intervals —
active moments followed by deep rest.

Today I nourish my body with:

_____

Today I move with intention through:

_____

JOURNAL REFLECTION

Where am I overdoing or under-being?
What brings balance back?
How can I hold peace while taking action?

_____

_____

"I honor the dance of effort and ease."

EVENING GRATITUDE

A moment of balance today:

_____

_____

TRUEJOY-LIVING

A YEAR OF TRANSFORMATION

DAY 308-Integration & Return — Living TrueJoy Daily

"My purpose is love in motion."

MORNING RITUAL

Whisper: "I remember why I began."
Review your original intention for transformation — breathe it back into your body.
(Reconnection renews commitment.)

_____

JOURNAL REFLECTION

Why did I start this journey?
How has my purpose evolved?
How will I carry it forward?

_____

_____

MEAL & MOVEMENT

Eat foods that uplift your energy. Move passionately — dance, walk briskly, or move with music that inspires.

Today I nourish my body with:

_____

Today I move with intention through:

_____

"My why lives within me."

EVENING GRATITUDE

A moment I felt purposeful:

_____

_____

DAY 309-Integration & Return —
Living TrueJoy Daily

"Becoming is lifelong; I am patient with my unfolding."

MORNING RITUAL

Whisper: "I am both masterpiece and
work in progress."
Spend a few moments in silence, simply
noticing your breath and being.
(Peace is found in patient evolution.)

_____

_____

MEAL & MOVEMENT

Eat something warm and nourishing. Move
softly — restorative stretches or a slow walk.

Today I nourish my body with:

_____

Today I move with intention through:

_____

JOURNAL REFLECTION

What am I still becoming?
How can I be patient with my process?
What feels complete for now?

_____

_____

"Becoming is enough."

EVENING GRATITUDE

A moment I trusted my timing:

_____

_____

TRUEJOY-LIVING
A YEAR OF TRANSFORMATION

DAY 310-Integration & Return — Living TrueJoy Daily

"Joy is no longer a goal — it's my way of being."

MORNING RITUAL

Whisper: "Today, I am TrueJoy."
Smile as you wake. Move with gratitude.
Speak with love. Live this day as a
reflection of who you've become.
(This is your integration in motion.)

MEAL & MOVEMENT

Eat intuitively and joyfully. Move naturally — your
body knows how to celebrate.

Today I nourish my body with:

Today I move with intention through:

JOURNAL REFLECTION

What does TrueJoy feel like for me now?
How can I live this daily?
What do I want to pass on to others?

"I am the embodiment of joy."

EVENING GRATITUDE

A moment I lived as TrueJoy today:

TRUEJOY-LIVING

A YEAR OF TRANSFORMATION

DAY 311-Integration & Return —
Living TrueJoy Daily

"Today I embody Light."

MORNING RITUAL

"Today I embody Light." (Choose a word — Peace, Grace, Joy, Flow, Trust, Light.) 3 breaths. Whisper your word. Carry it all day.

JOURNAL REFLECTION

How did I embody my word today?
Where did joy find me?
What reminded me of balance or love?

MEAL & MOVEMENT

Nourish and move in alignment with your energy.

Today I nourish my body with:

_____

Today I move with intention through:

_____

"I am whole. I am here. I am joy."

EVENING GRATITUDE

One thing I'm grateful for.
One thing I'll release before rest.

DAY 312-Integration & Return —
Living TrueJoy Daily

"Peace is not something I find — it's who I am when I am still."

MORNING RITUAL

Whisper: "I begin this day in calm presence."
Sit quietly for three deep breaths, noticing the space between each inhale and exhale.
(Peace begins with awareness.)

MEAL & MOVEMENT

Choose gentle nourishment — herbal tea, fruit, or warm oats. Move softly — stretching or slow yoga flow.

Today I nourish my body with:

_____

Today I move with intention through:

_____

JOURNAL REFLECTION

Where in my life do I need to bring more peace?
What disturbs my inner calm — and how can I release it?
What feels peaceful in my body right now?

_____

"I am a vessel of peace."

EVENING GRATITUDE

One peaceful moment I experienced today:

_____

DAY 313-Integration & Return —
Living TrueJoy Daily

"Grace flows through me when I let go of control."

MORNING RITUAL

Whisper: "Today, I move with grace."
Notice one moment of beauty around you —
light, air, sound — and breathe it in.
(Grace is the quiet rhythm of acceptance.)

MEAL & MOVEMENT

Eat lightly and gratefully. Move fluidly — slow
dance, gentle walking, or mindful movement.

Today I nourish my body with:

_____

Today I move with intention through:

_____

JOURNAL REFLECTION

What does grace mean to me today?
How can I show grace to myself and others?
What helps me soften into acceptance?

"I am held in grace."

EVENING GRATITUDE

One moment I chose grace instead of resistance:

_____

_____

DAY 314–Integration & Return —
Living TrueJoy Daily

"Joy is my natural state — I simply return to it."

MORNING RITUAL

Whisper: "Today, I choose joy in every breath."
Smile upon waking, stretch your arms wide, and feel joy fill your chest.
(Joy blooms when we stop searching for it.)

_____

_____

JOURNAL REFLECTION

What brings me genuine joy?
How can I cultivate joy through simple actions?
When was the last time I laughed deeply?

_____

_____

MEAL & MOVEMENT

Eat colorful foods that bring delight. Move playfully — dance, walk outdoors, or laugh freely.

Today I nourish my body with:

_____

Today I move with intention through:

_____

"Joy flows effortlessly through me."

EVENING GRATITUDE

A moment that sparked joy today:

_____

_____

TRUEJOY-LIVING
A YEAR OF TRANSFORMATION

DAY 315-Integration & Return — Living TrueJoy Daily

"When I surrender, life moves through me with ease."

MORNING RITUAL

Whisper: "I release control and trust the flow."
Imagine yourself floating gently downstream — supported, safe, guided.
(Flow begins where resistance ends.)

_____

_____

JOURNAL REFLECTION

Where am I resisting life's flow?
What does surrender feel like in my body?
How can I trust more deeply today?

_____

_____

MEAL & MOVEMENT

Eat intuitively — listen to what your body craves.
Move freely — fluid, rhythmic, unstructured.

Today I nourish my body with:

_____

Today I move with intention through:

_____

"I trust the rhythm of my life."

EVENING GRATITUDE
One thing that flowed easily today:

_____

_____

DAY 316-Integration & Return —
Living TrueJoy Daily

"I am guided by something greater — I trust the unfolding."

MORNING RITUAL

Whisper: "Everything is working out for my highest good."

Write or speak one area of life where you're ready to release fear.

(Trust transforms uncertainty into peace.)

JOURNAL REFLECTION

What area of life asks for my trust right now?

What happens when I stop forcing outcomes?

How does trust feel in my body?

MEAL & MOVEMENT

Choose grounding foods — root vegetables, grains. Move confidently — strong yoga poses, intentional walking.

Today I nourish my body with:

Today I move with intention through:

"I am supported in every step."

EVENING GRATITUDE

A moment I trusted instead of controlling:

TRUEJOY-LIVING

A YEAR OF TRANSFORMATION

DAY 317-Integration & Return — Living TrueJoy Daily

"My light shines brightest when I live authentically."

MORNING RITUAL

Whisper: "I bring light wherever I go."
Light a candle or sit near sunlight — feel
it warming your heart space.
(Light expands through authenticity.)

MEAL & MOVEMENT

Eat bright, colorful foods. Move with open posture — chest lifted, heart forward.

Today I nourish my body with:

_____

Today I move with intention through:

_____

JOURNAL REFLECTION

Where can I shine more freely?

What dims my inner light?

How can I illuminate others' paths today?

"My light is love made visible."

EVENING GRATITUDE

One way I brought light to the world today:

_____

_____

DAY 318-Integration & Return —
Living TrueJoy Daily
"Presence is the doorway to peace."

MORNING RITUAL
Whisper: "I am here now."
Pause before checking your phone or moving into the day.
Notice one sound, one scent, one sensation.
(Presence awakens gratitude for what already is.)

JOURNAL REFLECTION
What helps me return to presence?
How often do I move through the day unconsciously?
What anchors me in the moment?

MEAL & MOVEMENT
Eat slowly, savoring each bite. Move mindfully — notice how each step feels beneath you.

Today I nourish my body with:

_____

Today I move with intention through:

_____

"I am anchored in now."

EVENING GRATITUDE
A moment I felt fully present today:

_____

_____

DAY 319-Integration & Return —
Living TrueJoy Daily
"My heart opens wider each time I forgive."

MORNING RITUAL

Whisper: "I choose understanding over judgment."
Visualize a soft light expanding from your chest with every breath.
(Compassion dissolves walls and invites healing.)

MEAL & MOVEMENT

Eat something comforting. Move gently — yoga, stretching, or a mindful walk focusing on kindness toward yourself.

Today I nourish my body with:

_____

Today I move with intention through:

_____

JOURNAL REFLECTION

Where can I offer compassion today?
How can I soften my self-talk?
What does forgiveness feel like in my body?

"My heart is a safe place."

EVENING GRATITUDE

Someone or something I offered compassion to:

_____

_____

DAY 320-Integration & Return —
Living TrueJoy Daily

"I walk forward even when I can't see the path."

MORNING RITUAL

Whisper: "I am brave in becoming."
Write one fear you are ready to release.
(Courage is quiet commitment, not loud
force.)

_____

_____

JOURNAL REFLECTION

What fear am I ready to face?
How does courage feel in my body?
What act of bravery would honor me today?

_____

_____

MEAL & MOVEMENT

Eat energizing meals — protein, greens. Move
boldly — power walk or strong yoga flow.

Today I nourish my body with:

_____

Today I move with intention through:

_____

"I am strong in softness."

EVENING GRATITUDE

A moment I chose courage:

_____

_____

DAY 321-Integration & Return — Living TrueJoy Daily

"Balance is not perfection — it's presence in motion."

MORNING RITUAL

Whisper: "I move with harmony."
Alternate deep inhales and exhales,
feeling the symmetry.
(Balance lives in rhythm, not rigidity.)

MEAL & MOVEMENT

Eat in harmony — a mix of grounding and fresh foods. Move through yin-yang practice: effort ↠ ease.

Today I nourish my body with:

_____

Today I move with intention through:

_____

JOURNAL REFLECTION

Where do I need restoration?
What throws me off balance?
How can I return to center today?

_____

_____

"I honor the dance of balance."

EVENING GRATITUDE
A moment of equilibrium I felt today:

_____

_____

DAY 322-Integration & Return —
Living TrueJoy Daily
"Faith is trusting the unseen alignment."

MORNING RITUAL

Whisper: "I trust the path unfolding before me."
Spend a moment in stillness, imagining invisible hands guiding you.
(Faith bridges the gap between effort and surrender.)

_____

_____

JOURNAL REFLECTION

Where am I being asked to trust right now?
How does faith change my energy?
What proof has life already shown me that I am supported?

_____

_____

MEAL & MOVEMENT

Eat simply and gratefully. Move with eyes closed for a few moments to practice trust in body and breath.

Today I nourish my body with:

_____

Today I move with intention through:

_____

> *"I walk in faith."*

EVENING GRATITUDE

A moment I felt guided today:

_____

_____

TRUEJOY-LIVING
A YEAR OF TRANSFORMATION

DAY 323-Integration & Return — Living TrueJoy Daily

"My mind is clear when my heart is aligned."

MORNING RITUAL

Whisper: "I see truth through love."
Write down one decision you need clarity
on and breathe deeply.
(Clarity arrives in still waters.)

MEAL & MOVEMENT

Hydrate deeply, eat light. Move to clear energy —
walk in fresh air, stretch your spine.

Today I nourish my body with:

Today I move with intention through:

JOURNAL REFLECTION

What feels unclear right now?
How does my body signal yes vs no?
What truth am I ready to accept?

"My clarity is calm confidence."

EVENING GRATITUDE

Something became clear to me today:

DAY 324-Integration & Return —
Living TrueJoy Daily
"I trust the timing of my becoming."

MORNING RITUAL

Whisper: "I allow life to unfold."
Watch the sunrise or the movement of
your breath — both happen in perfect
timing.
(Patience is active trust.)

MEAL & MOVEMENT

Eat slowly. Move gently — tai chi or slow stretching
to sync with breath.

Today I nourish my body with:

_____

Today I move with intention through:

_____

JOURNAL REFLECTION

What am I rushing in my life?

What can I trust to take its time?

How does patience feel in my nervous system?

"Everything blooms in divine time."

EVENING GRATITUDE

A moment I chose patience:

_____

DAY 325-Integration & Return — Living TrueJoy Daily

"In letting go, I find freedom."

MORNING RITUAL

Whisper: "I release what no longer serves me."
Visualize old energies melting away like snow in sunlight.
(Surrender is the path of peace.)

MEAL & MOVEMENT

Eat clean and simple. Move freely — shake out the body and breathe deeply.

Today I nourish my body with:

_____

Today I move with intention through:

_____

JOURNAL REFLECTION

What am I ready to release?
How do I feel when I finally let go?
What new space does surrender create in me?

"I am free in trust."

EVENING GRATITUDE
Something I released today:

_____

_____

DAY 326-Integration & Return —
Living TrueJoy Daily

"I am a constant expression of new beginnings."

MORNING RITUAL

Whisper: "I welcome the freshness of today."

Open a window, inhale deeply, and feel the air cleanse your energy.

(Renewal is life's natural pulse.)

_____

_____

MEAL & MOVEMENT

Eat vibrant foods — greens and citrus. Move briskly or walk outdoors to invite revival.

Today I nourish my body with:

_____

Today I move with intention through:

_____

JOURNAL REFLECTION

What feels ready to be renewed?

How can I invite fresh energy into my routine?

What old belief am I ready to release?

_____

_____

"I am always becoming."

EVENING GRATITUDE

Something that felt new today:

_____

_____

DAY 327-Integration & Return —
Living TrueJoy Daily

"Every moment mirrors my inner state."

MORNING RITUAL

Whisper: "I see myself with clarity and kindness."
Gaze into a mirror and smile without judgment.
(Reflection reveals truth gently.)

MEAL & MOVEMENT

Choose balanced meals. Move slowly — yin yoga or stretching.

Today I nourish my body with:

Today I move with intention through:

JOURNAL REFLECTION

What am I learning from my own patterns?
Where have I grown the most?
What truth is ready to be seen?

"I am a student of my own wisdom."

EVENING GRATITUDE

One insight I gained today:

DAY 328-Integration & Return — Living TrueJoy Daily

"I am woven into a greater whole."

MORNING RITUAL

Whisper: "I connect with life through love."
Reach out to someone today or send a silent blessing.
(Connection is communion with everything.)

MEAL & MOVEMENT

Share a meal if possible. Move with others — walk, dance, or join a class.

Today I nourish my body with:

_____

Today I move with intention through:

_____

JOURNAL REFLECTION

Who am I grateful to have in my life?
How does connection nourish me?
Where can I offer more presence in relationship?

"I belong to love."

_____

EVENING GRATITUDE
A connection I honored today:

_____

_____

DAY 329-Integration & Return — Living TrueJoy Daily

"Creation flows through me effortlessly."

MORNING RITUAL

Whisper: "I open to inspiration."
Write or sketch freely for ten minutes without editing.
(Creativity is divine play.)

MEAL & MOVEMENT

Eat colorfully. Move expressively — dance or paint with your body.

Today I nourish my body with:

_____

Today I move with intention through:

_____

JOURNAL REFLECTION

What wants to be created through me?
How do I block inspiration?
Where can I allow more play?

"I am a channel of creation."

EVENING GRATITUDE
Something I created today:

_____

_____

DAY 330-Integration & Return — Living TrueJoy Daily

"When I align with truth, life flows easily."

MORNING RITUAL

Whisper: "I choose what feels true."
Place a hand over your heart and ask,
"What feels aligned today?"
(Alignment is honoring inner yes.)

MEAL & MOVEMENT

Eat mindfully. Move organically — walk or stretch where it feels good.

Today I nourish my body with:

_____

Today I move with intention through:

_____

JOURNAL REFLECTION

What feels in or out of alignment?
How does my body signal truth?
What small adjustment brings ease?

_____

_____

"I am in harmony with life."

EVENING GRATITUDE

One aligned choice I made:

_____

_____

DAY 331-Integration & Return —
Living TrueJoy Daily

"I find beauty in the space between steps."

MORNING RITUAL

Whisper: "I walk slowly and see clearly."
Take a five-minute walk without
destination.
(Patience grows through presence.)

MEAL & MOVEMENT

Eat warm, soothing meals. Move slow and steady.

Today I nourish my body with:

_____

Today I move with intention through:

_____

JOURNAL REFLECTION

What can wait today?
Where do I rush past joy?
How can I breathe between moments?

"I honor divine timing."

EVENING GRATITUDE
A moment I paused gratefully:

_____

_____

DAY 332-Integration & Return — Living TrueJoy Daily

"Nothing is missing — I am complete as I am."

MORNING RITUAL

Whisper: "I embrace all of me."
List three traits you once judged but now see as part of your wholeness.
(Wholeness is acceptance in action.)

_____

JOURNAL REFLECTION

What parts of me need more love?
How does wholeness feel in my body?
What reminds me I am complete?

_____

_____

MEAL & MOVEMENT

Eat nourishing, balanced meals. Move through a full-body stretch sequence.

Today I nourish my body with:

_____

Today I move with intention through:

_____

"I am whole and holy."

EVENING GRATITUDE

Something I accepted about myself:

_____

_____

DAY 333-Integration & Return — Living TrueJoy Daily

"I let go of what weighs me down."

MORNING RITUAL

Whisper: "I breathe in light."
Stretch your arms up, inhale freedom,
and release a sigh.
(Lightness is liberation from
overthinking.)

MEAL & MOVEMENT

Eat fresh and simple. Move playfully — dance or
bounce to music.

Today I nourish my body with:

_____

Today I move with intention through:

_____

JOURNAL REFLECTION

What burden am I ready to set down?
How can I bring more play into today?
What thought can I replace with laughter?

"I am free to float in joy."

EVENING GRATITUDE
A moment I felt light:

_____

_____

DAY 334-Integration & Return — Living TrueJoy Daily

"My actions honor my truth."

MORNING RITUAL

Whisper: "I act from alignment."
Review your plans and remove anything
that feels forced.
(Integrity is self-respect in motion.)

MEAL & MOVEMENT

Eat clean foods. Move decisively — stand tall and
confident.

Today I nourish my body with:

Today I move with intention through:

JOURNAL REFLECTION

Where am I out of alignment with my values?
What small action restores integrity?
How does honesty feel in my body?

"I am true to my essence."

EVENING GRATITUDE

An honest moment today:

DAY 335-Integration & Return —
Living TrueJoy Daily

"Kindness is my default setting."

MORNING RITUAL

Whisper: "May my words heal today."
Send a loving text or speak kindly to
yourself in the mirror.

MEAL & MOVEMENT

Share food or gratitude with someone. Move with
compassion for your body.

Today I nourish my body with:

_____

Today I move with intention through:

_____

JOURNAL REFLECTION

Who needs kindness from me today?
How does kindness shift my energy?
Where can I be gentler with myself?

"My heart radiates gentleness."

EVENING GRATITUDE
A kind moment I shared:

_____

_____

DAY 336-Integration & Return —
Living TrueJoy Daily

"My truth is my power."

MORNING RITUAL

Whisper: "I show up as myself."
Take a deep breath and release the need
to please.
(Authenticity is the purest form of
freedom.)

MEAL & MOVEMENT

Eat what feels right for you. Move in a way that
feels real — not performed.

Today I nourish my body with:

_____

Today I move with intention through:

_____

JOURNAL REFLECTION

Where am I pretending to be something I'm not?
How does authenticity feel in my body?
What truth am I ready to express?

"I am safe in my truth"

EVENING GRATITUDE

A moment I was unapologetically me:

_____

_____

DAY 337-Integration & Return —
Living TrueJoy Daily

"Love flows freely through my thoughts, words, and actions."

MORNING RITUAL

Whisper: "I choose love in every interaction."
Place a hand over your heart, breathe warmth into your chest, and visualize light expanding outward.

MEAL & MOVEMENT

Eat something prepared with care. Move gently — stretch or walk while focusing on your heartbeat.

Today I nourish my body with:

Today I move with intention through:

JOURNAL REFLECTION

How can I embody love more today?
Who needs compassion from me?
What does unconditional love feel like?

"Love begins with me."

EVENING GRATITUDE

A moment I gave or received love:

DAY 338-Integration & Return — Living TrueJoy Daily

"When I listen, I connect with truth."

MORNING RITUAL

Whisper: "I listen with presence."
Spend five minutes in silence — notice sounds, your breath, your heartbeat.
What does my inner voice want to say?

MEAL & MOVEMENT

Eat quietly, savoring each flavor. Move slowly — pay attention to how your body feels.

Today I nourish my body with:

_____

Today I move with intention through:

_____

JOURNAL REFLECTION

Where can I listen more deeply?
How does stillness speak to me?

"I hear the wisdom within."

_____

_____

EVENING GRATITUDE

Something I learned by listening:

_____

_____

TRUEJOY-LIVING

A YEAR OF TRANSFORMATION

DAY 339-Integration & Return — Living TrueJoy Daily

"My freedom comes from authenticity."

MORNING RITUAL

Whisper: "I release what limits me." Breathe deeply and visualize old constraints melting away. Where in life do I feel most alive?

JOURNAL REFLECTION

What belief or habit can I release? How do I define freedom?

MEAL & MOVEMENT

Eat what feels liberating, not habitual. Move with openness — stretch, dance, or walk outside.

Today I nourish my body with:

_____

Today I move with intention through:

_____

"I am free to be me."

EVENING GRATITUDE

One moment of liberation today:

_____

TRUEJOY-LIVING

A YEAR OF TRANSFORMATION

DAY 340-Integration & Return —
Living TrueJoy Daily

"Simplicity opens space for peace."

MORNING RITUAL

Whisper: "I choose ease."
Declutter one space — desk, bag, or
mind. What can I simplify today?

JOURNAL REFLECTION

How does simplicity make me feel?
What am I holding onto that adds weight?

MEAL & MOVEMENT

Eat fresh and minimal. Move gently — stretch or
take a mindful walk.

Today I nourish my body with:

_____

Today I move with intention through:

_____

"Less is more peace."

EVENING GRATITUDE
Something simple that brought joy:

_____

_____

DAY 341-Integration & Return — Living TrueJoy Daily

"Playfulness reconnects me to joy."

MORNING RITUAL

Whisper: "I allow fun today."
Do something spontaneous or silly.
Laugh freely. How can I invite laughter into my day?

_____

_____

JOURNAL REFLECTION

When did I last play for no reason?
What makes me feel carefree?

_____

MEAL & MOVEMENT

Eat something colorful. Move playfully — dance, skip, or sway.

Today I nourish my body with:

_____

Today I move with intention through:

_____

"Joy is my nature."

EVENING GRATITUDE

A playful moment I enjoyed:

_____

_____

DAY 342-Integration & Return —
Living TrueJoy Daily

"In stillness, I find everything I seek."

MORNING RITUAL

Whisper: "I am calm and clear."
Sit quietly for five minutes, noticing breath and space. What happens when I am still?

MEAL & MOVEMENT

Eat slowly. Move softly — gentle yoga or mindful stretching.

Today I nourish my body with:

Today I move with intention through:

JOURNAL REFLECTION

Where do I resist rest?

How can I listen more deeply to silence?

"I rest in serenity."

EVENING GRATITUDE
A moment of peace today:

TRUEJOY-LIVING
A YEAR OF TRANSFORMATION

DAY 343-Integration & Return — Living TrueJoy Daily

"I trust my voice and my vision."

MORNING RITUAL

Whisper: "I walk tall in my truth."
List three things you're proud of — say them aloud. What am I proud of today?

JOURNAL REFLECTION

How does confidence feel physically?

Where can I show up boldly?

MEAL & MOVEMENT

Eat strong, energizing foods. Move powerfully — stand tall, breathe deeply.

Today I nourish my body with:

_____

Today I move with intention through:

_____

"I am enough."

EVENING GRATITUDE

A moment I stood in my power:

_____

_____

DAY 344-Integration & Return —
Living TrueJoy Daily
"My purpose is expressed through presence."

MORNING RITUAL

Whisper: "I live my purpose naturally."
Write what you feel called to contribute
today. What feels purposeful today?

MEAL & MOVEMENT

Eat with intention. Move purposefully — step,
breathe, act with awareness.

Today I nourish my body with:

_____

Today I move with intention through:

_____

JOURNAL REFLECTION

What gives my life meaning?

How do I express my gifts?

"I am living my why."

EVENING GRATITUDE

One aligned action I took:

_____

_____

DAY 345-Integration & Return —
Living TrueJoy Daily
"I move with the rhythm of life."

MORNING RITUAL

Whisper: "I am in tune with today."
Take three breaths and imagine harmony
filling you. What feels harmonious today?

JOURNAL REFLECTION

Where can I bring balance?
How can I flow with grace?

MEAL & MOVEMENT

Eat a balanced meal. Move fluidly — music or
flowing yoga.

Today I nourish my body with:

Today I move with intention through:

"I am aligned with life's song."

EVENING GRATITUDE

A moment that felt harmonious:

DAY 346-Integration & Return —
Living TrueJoy Daily

"I already have everything I need."

MORNING RITUAL

Whisper: "I notice the abundance around me."
List five blessings before starting your day.

MEAL & MOVEMENT

Eat generously, share if possible. Move expansively — arms wide, open-hearted.

Today I nourish my body with:

_____

Today I move with intention through:

_____

JOURNAL REFLECTION

What abundance surrounds me?
Where can I give more?
What am I grateful for today?

"I am open to receive."

EVENING GRATITUDE

Something abundant in my life:

_____

_____

DAY 347-Integration & Return — Living TrueJoy Daily

"Every moment is an invitation to be aware."

MORNING RITUAL

Whisper: "I choose to notice."
As you get ready, pay attention to each action fully. How can I be more mindful today?

JOURNAL REFLECTION

What moments did I miss by rushing?
What does awareness feel like?

MEAL & MOVEMENT

Eat slowly and consciously. Move in silence — observe each motion.

Today I nourish my body with:

Today I move with intention through:

"Awareness is peace."

EVENING GRATITUDE

A mindful moment today:

DAY 348-Integration & Return —
Living TrueJoy Daily

"My intuition is sacred guidance."

MORNING RITUAL

Whisper: "I trust my inner knowing."
Ask your intuition one question — write
the first answer that comes.

_____

JOURNAL REFLECTION

What message is my intuition sending?
How can I honor it more?
When do I feel my inner yes?

_____
_____

MEAL & MOVEMENT

Eat what feels right, not what's routine. Move
freely — follow impulse.

Today I nourish my body with:

_____

Today I move with intention through:

_____

"I am guided from within."

EVENING GRATITUDE

A moment I trusted my intuition:

_____
_____

DAY 349–Begin Again
"I move with calm purpose."

MORNING RITUAL

Whisper: "I act from center, not from urgency."
Before starting tasks, pause for three breaths and feel grounded. How can I bring peace into productivity?

JOURNAL REFLECTION

Where can I slow down yet still progress?
What does calm action feel like?

MEAL & MOVEMENT

Eat a steady, balanced meal. Move with control — slow stretches or a mindful walk between tasks.

Today I nourish my body with:

Today I move with intention through:

"I achieve through ease."

EVENING GRATITUDE
One action that felt peaceful:

DAY 350–Begin Again

"Gratitude transforms the ordinary into sacred."

MORNING RITUAL

Whisper: "I see beauty in everything."
Write three things you appreciate about
this morning.

MEAL & MOVEMENT

Eat with mindfulness — notice texture and taste.
Move gently as you reflect on thankfulness.

Today I nourish my body with:

_____

Today I move with intention through:

_____

JOURNAL REFLECTION

What am I most thankful for right now?

How does gratitude shift my energy?

Who can I thank today?

"Thank you for this day."

EVENING GRATITUDE

Something I appreciated today:

_____

_____

DAY 351–Begin Again

"I rise stronger after every storm."

MORNING RITUAL

Whisper: "I bend, but I do not break."
Reflect on a past challenge and the
strength it gave you.

JOURNAL REFLECTION

What have I overcome?

How did I heal?

What does resilience look like in me?

MEAL & MOVEMENT

Eat nourishing foods rich in color. Move steadily
— build strength with intention.

Today I nourish my body with:

Today I move with intention through:

"I am unshakable in grace."

EVENING GRATITUDE

A moment I proved my strength:

DAY 352–Begin Again

"I see clearly with open eyes and heart."

MORNING RITUAL

Whisper: "I welcome new awareness."
Notice something you've never seen
before in your space. Write about it.

MEAL & MOVEMENT

Eat fresh fruits or greens. Move in sunlight —
open arms wide.

Today I nourish my body with:

_____

Today I move with intention through:

_____

JOURNAL REFLECTION

What new truth am I seeing?

How does awareness change my choices?

What is awakening within me?

"I am awake to life."

EVENING GRATITUDE
A realization I had today:

_____

DAY 353–Begin Again

"My love for myself sets the tone for my world."

MORNING RITUAL

Whisper: "I treat myself with tenderness."
Place your hand on your heart and say, "I am enough." What makes me feel worthy?

JOURNAL REFLECTION

How did I honor myself today?
Where can I show more self-compassion?

MEAL & MOVEMENT

Eat what nourishes body and soul. Move kindly — stretch without judgment.

Today I nourish my body with:

Today I move with intention through:

"I am my own beloved."

EVENING GRATITUDE

One thing I love about myself:

DAY 354–Begin Again

"My inner voice is ancient and wise."

MORNING RITUAL

Whisper: "I trust my knowing."
Journal a question and let intuition
answer freely.

JOURNAL REFLECTION

What truth is surfacing today?

How does wisdom speak to me?

What guidance have I ignored?

MEAL & MOVEMENT

Eat simple foods. Move meditatively — slow steps
or flowing yoga.

Today I nourish my body with:

Today I move with intention through:

"I listen within."

EVENING GRATITUDE
A moment of clarity today:

TRUEJOY-LIVING

A YEAR OF TRANSFORMATION

DAY 355–Begin Again

"When my heart is clear, my path is simple."

MORNING RITUAL

Whisper: "I see through love."
Place a hand over your heart and breathe into truth. What does my heart want to say?

_____

JOURNAL REFLECTION

Where am I overthinking?
What brings me emotional clarity?

_____

_____

MEAL & MOVEMENT

Eat light foods. Move with focus — clear mind, soft heart.

Today I nourish my body with:

_____

Today I move with intention through:

_____

"My heart knows the way."

EVENING GRATITUDE
A heartfelt truth I honored:

_____

_____

TRUEJOY-LIVING

DAY 356–Begin Again
"I believe joy always returns."

MORNING RITUAL

Whisper: "I expect good things."
Smile as you breathe in hope. Where do I
need more faith?

_____

_____

JOURNAL REFLECTION

How can I welcome joy back in?
What reminds me to trust life's goodness?

_____

_____

MEAL & MOVEMENT

Eat something that uplifts you. Move lightly —
walk with optimism.

Today I nourish my body with:

_____

Today I move with intention through:

_____

"Joy always finds me."

EVENING GRATITUDE
A joyful moment today:

_____

_____

TRUEJOY-LIVING

A YEAR OF TRANSFORMATION

DAY 357-Begin Again

"Life supports me when I relax into it."

MORNING RITUAL

Whisper: "I am safe to trust."
Breathe out control and inhale peace.
What proof has life already given me?

MEAL & MOVEMENT

Eat calmly. Move fluidly — gentle yoga or nature walk.

Today I nourish my body with:

_____

Today I move with intention through:

_____

JOURNAL REFLECTION

What am I ready to trust?
How does trust change my energy?

"I am awake to life."

EVENING GRATITUDE
Something that worked out today:

_____

_____

DAY 358–Begin Again

"I shed the old and welcome the new."

MORNING RITUAL

Whisper: "I am ready for renewal."
Write one habit or thought to release
today.

_____

_____

JOURNAL REFLECTION

What part of me is being reborn?
How do I welcome change?
What does new energy feel like?

_____

_____

MEAL & MOVEMENT

Eat cleansing foods. Move freely — stretch or
shake off tension.

Today I nourish my body with:

_____

Today I move with intention through:

_____

"I am ever becoming."

EVENING GRATITUDE

Something I let go of today:

_____

_____

DAY 359–Begin Again

"My light inspires others to shine."

MORNING RITUAL

Whisper: "I shine brightly and softly."
Stand in sunlight or imagine it flowing
through you.

JOURNAL REFLECTION

What part of me is being reborn?
How do I welcome change?
What does new energy feel like?

MEAL & MOVEMENT

Eat cleansing foods. Move freely — stretch or
shake off tension.

Today I nourish my body with:

Today I move with intention through:

"I am the light I seek."

EVENING GRATITUDE

A moment I felt radiant:

DAY 360-Begin Again

"Contentment is my natural state."

MORNING RITUAL

Whisper: "I have enough, I am enough."
Savor your morning slowly and fully.
What feels complete in my life?

MEAL & MOVEMENT

Eat your favorite meal mindfully. Move with gratitude for your body.

Today I nourish my body with:

_____

Today I move with intention through:

_____

JOURNAL REFLECTION

How can I enjoy this moment more?
What is already perfect as it is?

"I am whole and satisfied."

EVENING GRATITUDE

One thing that fulfilled me today:

_____

_____

DAY 361–Begin Again
"I am one with all that is."

MORNING RITUAL

Whisper: "I belong to this moment."
Visualize yourself as part of nature's
web. When do I feel most connected to
life?

JOURNAL REFLECTION

How can I contribute to the whole?
What does unity mean to me?

MEAL & MOVEMENT

Eat sustainably. Move outdoors if possible.

Today I nourish my body with:

Today I move with intention through:

"I am part of everything."

EVENING GRATITUDE

A connection I honored today:

DAY 362–Begin Again

"My presence is healing."

MORNING RITUAL

Whisper: "I bring calm where I go."
Spend a moment sending kind thoughts
to someone in need. What does
compassion look like today?

_____

_____

JOURNAL REFLECTION

Who benefits from my presence?
How can I be more empathetic?

_____

_____

MEAL & MOVEMENT

Eat soft, nourishing foods. Move slowly — gentle
breathing and open hands.

Today I nourish my body with:

_____

Today I move with intention through:

_____

_____

"My presence is love in motion."

EVENING GRATITUDE

A moment I brought peace to someone:

_____

_____

DAY 363-Begin Again

"All I have learned lives within me."

MORNING RITUAL

Whisper: "I carry my wisdom forward."
Review your favorite lesson from this
journey.

MEAL & MOVEMENT

Eat a meal that feels nourishing and familiar.
Move in gratitude for your growth.

Today I nourish my body with:

_____

Today I move with intention through:

_____

JOURNAL REFLECTION

What have I mastered?

How do I embody balance?

What will I continue to practice?

"I am integration in motion."

EVENING GRATITUDE

A teaching that stayed with me:

_____

_____

DAY 364–Begin Again

"I honor how far I've come."

MORNING RITUAL

Whisper: "I celebrate my journey."
Dance, smile, or speak gratitude aloud.
How has this year transformed me?

MEAL & MOVEMENT

Eat something you love. Move freely —
celebratory and joyful.

Today I nourish my body with:

_____

Today I move with intention through:

_____

JOURNAL REFLECTION

What am I most proud of?
Who helped me along the way?

"I am grateful for every step."

EVENING GRATITUDE

One achievement I celebrate:

_____

_____

DAY 365-Begin Again

"Every ending is the beginning of a deeper becoming."

MORNING RITUAL

Whisper: "I start anew, with gratitude and grace."
Revisit your Day 1 entry — notice who you've become and set one intention for your next chapter.

MEAL & MOVEMENT

Eat your favorite grounding meal. Move with reverence — a final reflection walk or stretch of gratitude.

Today I nourish my body with:

_____

Today I move with intention through:

_____

JOURNAL REFLECTION

How has this year changed me?
What am I ready to carry forward?
What will my next cycle of growth look like?

*"I am infinite transformation.
I am TrueJoy."*

EVENING GRATITUDE

The most important lesson I've learned:

_____

Thank You for Journeying
Through a Year of Transformation

You have done something extraordinary.

You showed up — day after day, page after page —to nurture your mind, body, and soul.

This journal was never about perfection — it was about presence. You learned to trust your rhythm, to soften into the flow of becoming, and to live your life as the sacred ritual it is.

Your transformation doesn't end here — it expands. Every morning you wake, you begin again.

Reflection

What changed within you this year?

What wisdom will you carry forward?

What does TrueJoy mean to you now?

Take a deep breath. Smile. You are not who you were when you began. You are lighter, clearer, truer — and infinitely more you.

Keep your rituals alive.
Return to the practices that ground and uplift you. Let joy, awareness, and intention continue to guide your path.

You are TrueJoy Living.
You are the embodiment of transformation.

Transformation is not a destination — it's a rhythm. Every breath, every choice, every dawn is another chance to rise.

With Deep Gratitude,

Joy Hafner
Founder, TrueJoy-Living
Guiding you to live aligned, grounded, and free.

TRUEJOY-LIVING
A YEAR OF TRANSFORMATION

FINAL BLESSING

As you come to the end of this year-long journey, may you feel the quiet strength that has grown within you — the strength that comes not from striving, but from listening. Not from perfection, but from presence. Not from doing more, but from honoring what is true for you.

May you trust the wisdom you've uncovered.
May you stand gently but firmly in your inner knowing.
May you follow the rhythm of your own becoming with compassion, devotion, and grace.

You have shown up for yourself in ways that matter.
You have chosen awareness over autopilot.
You have chosen alignment over urgency.
You have chosen yourself, page after page, moment after moment.

Carry what you've learned here into the days ahead:
✨ Move with intention.
✨ Speak with clarity.
✨ Rest when your soul asks.
✨ Create from your heart.
✨ Release what weighs you down.
✨ Return to your center whenever you drift away.

May this year of reflection open a deeper relationship with yourself — one built on trust, tenderness, and truth. And may you continue, with courage and openness, to master the greatest art of all: the art of being wholly, authentically you. With love, presence, and gratitude, May your next chapter be your most aligned yet.